THE CRISIS IN MORAL TEACHING
in the Episcopal Church

Edited by

Timothy F. Sedgwick

and

Philip Turner

MOREHOUSE PUBLISHING
Harrisburg, PA

Morehouse Publishing
P.O. Box 1321
Harrisburg, PA 17105

Library of Congress Cataloging-in-Publication Data
    The Crisis in moral teaching in the Episcopal Church / edited by Timothy F. Sedgwick and Philip Turner.
        p.   cm.
    Includes bibliographical references.
    Contents: Decorum as doctrine / Harmon L. Smith—New technologies for assisted reproduction / David H. Smith, Judith A. Granbois—Changing teachings on abortion / David A. Scott—The economic order / Timothy F. Sedgwick—On war, peace, and the use of force / Allan M. Parrent—The dispersal of moral authority / Ellen K. Wondra—How the church might teach / Philip Turner.
    ISBN 0-8192-1592-9
    1. Episcopal Church—Doctrines.   2. Anglican Communion—Doctrines.   3. Episcopal Church—Teaching office.   4. Anglican Communion—Teaching office.   5. Christian ethics—Anglican authors. I. Sedgwick, Timothy F.   II. Turner, Philip, 1935–
BX5930.2.C75   1992   92-21582
241'.04373—dc20   CIP

Printed in the United States of America
by
BSC Litho
Harrisburg, PA 17105

10 9 8 7 6 5 4 3 2

Second Printing, 1994

Contents

To Charles Perry

for his fidelity to the Church
from which this work is born.

Acknowledgments

In 1988 a group of professors of Christian ethics met at the National Cathedral in Washington, D.C., to share something of their work and concerns as theologians of the church. This meeting began a series of conversations among the members of this group and with several bishops on moral teachings in the Episcopal Church. The conversations issued, in time, in the studies for this volume.

None of these things could have happened without the generosity of a number of people and institutions. The Very Rev. Charles Perry, then provost at the National Cathedral, was a gracious host and participant in this work. The National Cathedral generously helped to cover the expenses of these meetings. A grant from the Lilly Foundation also made possible the three meetings at the National Cathedral. A final consultation in Evanston, Illinois, to present publicly the studies and to begin work on bringing them to publication, was made possible by Seabury-Western Theological Seminary through the Bishop George Craig Stewart Lecture series.

Beyond the contributors to this volume, the conversation was informed through the participation of the Rev. John Archer, Bishop Mark Dyer, Bishop Ronald Haines, the Rev. Robert Hood, and Bishop Peter Lee.

List of Contributors

Judith A. Granbois
Program Associate
The Poynter Center
Indiana University

Allan M. Parrent
Associate Dean for Academic Affairs
The Clinton S. Quin Professor of Christian Ethics
Vice President
Virginia Theological Seminary

The Rev. David A. Scott
The William Meade Professor of Theology
Professor of Ethics
Virginia Theological Seminary

Timothy F. Sedgwick
Professor of Ethics and Moral Theology
Seabury-Western Theological Seminary

David H. Smith
Director, The Poynter Center
Professor of Religious Studies
Indiana University

The Rev. Harmon L. Smith
Professor of Christian Ethics
The Divinity School
Duke University

The Very Rev. Philip Turner
President and Dean
Professor of Christian Ethics
Berkeley Divinity School at Yale

The Rev. Ellen K. Wondra
Assistant Professor of Theology
Colgate-Rochester Divinity School/
Bexley Hall/Crozer Theological Seminary

Introduction

Timothy F. Sedgwick

This study of the Episcopal Church and its moral teachings arises from a sustained conversation among the eight contributors. Charles Perry, then dean and provost at the National Cathedral in Washington, D.C., and now dean of the Church Divinity School of the Pacific, hosted the first meeting in December 1988. At that meeting those gathered shared something of their work and concerns as theologians of the church.

The group did not reflect a singular moral outlook or stance. Broadly speaking, the theologians who have contributed to this volume range in their response to specific issues from what is normally viewed as moderately conservative to moderately liberal. Other differences include age, educational setting (some teach at universities and others at Episcopal seminaries), and training (contributors received their doctorates in theology and ethics from five different doctoral programs). Despite such differences, all share a common understanding of the discipline of Christian ethics and moral theology. Differences in moral judgments are not simply or narrowly matters of right and wrong. Rather, differences in judgment reflect differences in understandings that can be articulated, respected, and debated. Christian ethics and moral theology are disciplines designed to aid in this task.

For example, Christians through the ages have made different judgments about the use of military force. One person may stand within the pacifist tradition which sees God as calling for a nonviolent witness to the world. Another person may stand within the tradition of just war, which views God as calling upon them to exercise a worldly vocation to protect innocent human life through the use of force. Alternatively, two people may stand within the just war tradition but disagree whether military force is justified in a particular situa-

9

tion. They may disagree, for example, as to whether the cause is just, or whether there is a reasonable chance of success in waging war. Disagreements may stem from the facts of the situation, as well as from moral judgment regarding those facts.

As this example suggests, the contributors to this volume may disagree about a number of particular moral judgments. The reasons for differences in judgments may be theological, moral, factual, or some combination of these factors. These differences are not narrowly matters of truth and error. Reasonable, faithful people may reasonably and faithfully disagree about important moral issues. What the discipline of Christian ethics and moral theology provides is a framework in which to articulate and understand the basis for moral judgments. In this light, Christian ethics and moral theology provide the basis for critical reflection that informs moral judgments and promotes respect for those who may differ.

The contributors agree, however, that there are limits to disagreements among Christians. That is to say, while there are reasons for moral judgments, those reasons are limited. To use the example of military force again, advocating a holy war is immoral because innocent life is disregarded and sacrificed for the sake of some higher purpose. In such a crusade, the innocent are treated as means to some greater, holy end. God is assumed to command and support the particular aims of a people as holy and therefore to warrant an all-out war, including the taking of innocent life. Christians have concluded that such a use of military force cannot be justified morally or theologically.

Given differences in moral judgments, the contributors to this volume are concerned with how Christian moral teachings could and should both respect differences in moral judgments and identify the limits to such differences. In this light, all saw as inadequate current attempts on the part of the Episcopal Church in the United States of America (ECUSA) to formulate moral teachings. Individual statements, resolutions from General Convention, reports from standing committees and commissions, pastoral letters from bishops, studies from the national church—these and other works addressing moral issues produce a cacophony that appears to have no bounds and to respect no differences. Instead of teaching, the church increasingly yields to strident, ideological debates.

Failure to develop moral teachings that would inform Christians to respect differences in conscience and to provide clear witness to the world is not new. From the first conversations in 1988, and in subsequent meetings, the contributors to this book often recalled Paul Ramsey's 1967 book, *Who Speaks for the Church?*[1] Similarly, in 1978 James Gustafson described the crisis of moral teaching in Protestant churches as "only a little short of chaos."[2] Philip Turner aptly describes the problem by expanding Ramsey's question and asking, "Who speaks for the church to whom on what? Why? And how?"

Because these questions about the task and nature of moral teaching have not been adequately addressed, the authors of these essays have come to believe that the ability of ECUSA to offer moral guidance is in jeopardy. They decided that, in order to test their perception, they needed to work together over an extended period on a study of how the church has addressed specific moral issues. A legitimate assessment could then be made about the adequacy of ECUSA's work in moral teaching.

Five persons agreed to address five specific moral issues: human sexuality, birth technologies, abortion, the justice of the economic order, and the use of military force. The body of this volume is the result of those studies. The five cases are first of all descriptive presentations that provide a reading of what the church has taught in these areas.[3] They are also critical assessments of whether there is a common sense of purpose in the church's teachings and a consistency in the development of what is taught. Broader assessments are also made regarding the adequacy of the teachings themselves. These judgments reflect the individual judgments of the authors, but they stem from a common understanding that moral teachings depend upon arguments that are theological, moral, and factual. Finally, each author offers constructive suggestions, not narrowly in terms of what should be taught, but broadly in terms of what is necessary for the church to teach at all.

Some of the reasons for choosing these five issues suggest something further of the value of the case studies. Abortion, for example, is a moral issue which deeply divides the church and about which much has been said. How the church addresses an issue about which there are deep conflicts of conscience provides a good opportunity to illumine understandings of the task of moral teachings.

The study of teachings on human sexuality furthers the understanding of what is needed in the development of moral teachings. In addition to questions that focus on specific forms of sexual behavior, sexual ethics necessarily addresses broader questions both about the meaning of human sexuality and about the ways in which sexual practices may reflect and witness to Christian belief. Thus the debates over sexual ethics illumine the task of moral theology beyond the investigation of particular moral quandries and disputed judgments.

In part, birth technologies were chosen for study because they provide new moral choices and challenge the church to consider when and how to address issues that cannot be understood apart from the comprehension of a range of evolving, complex scientific data. The possibilities raised by new birth technologies poignantly raise the question, "Who needs to inform what is taught, and who is to teach?"

Moral teachings on the economic order and on the use of military force were chosen as the final two case studies. These two issues are more broadly social and political. They raise questions about the purpose and possibility of government and, more specifically, about the appropriate or just means for achieving the ends sought. Perhaps more than any other issue, teachings on the economic order reflect the church's understanding of Christian faith and its relationship to culture. In turn, teachings on the economic order provide a good case to assess the extent of the cultural captivity of the church. Finally, given the classic pacifist and just war stances within Christianity, the use of force again highlights the question of how the church should teach where faithful Christians have long disagreed about what should be done.

In the concluding essay in this volume, Philip Turner asks the question, "Who speaks for the church to whom on what? Why? And how?" The six questions Turner raises, in fact, suggest something of the constructive questions that each of the five case studies address.

1. On which issues is the church obliged to speak and why?

2. What ought to be the aim of moral teachings: prophetic pronouncement or the informing of conscience on issues on which faithful persons may disagree?

3. To whom ought the church address its statements: members of the church, policy makers, the general public?

4. What language should the church use in its teach-

ings in order to witness to the gospel and speak to "all persons of goodwill?"

5. What form ought the church to use in its teachings: resolutions, pastoral letters, canon law, the commissioning of studies by informed groups or persons?

6. Who ought to formulate and articulate the teachings of the church: bishops, General Convention, standing committees, trained theologians and ethicists, interested persons?

Again, regardless of personal convictions and judgments, the contributors to this volume agreed that these six questions must be addressed and answered if the church is to develop moral teachings that are something more than occasional, ad hoc, and contradictory statements.

A final introductory word is in order. These studies and the two concluding essays are addressed to the church-at-large, but especially to those who represent the church on its councils, commissions, and committees. Above all, the challenge of developing the moral teachings of the church is a challenge to the bishops in general and the House of Bishops in particular. This is necessarily so because a central task of the episcopate is teaching. As articulated in the ordination vows, bishops are to "guard the faith, unity, and discipline of the Church," (BCP, p. 518). However, the emphasis of these studies on developing moral teachings will be misconstrued if they are understood as a conservative attempt to gain integrity amidst the pluralism of the age through an ecclesial politics of definition and discipline.

In clearly defining the moral demands of Christian faith there is the basis for discipline, even if primarily self-discipline in which individuals will define themselves in or outside of the church, given the church's self-understanding. And certainly it is true that any attempt to articulate moral teachings involves some definition of what stands within and what stands outside of Christian identity. But these studies are equally interested in providing an informed basis for moral judgments and thereby in supporting and respecting diverse persons in the forming of their conscience. As Ellen Wondra emphasizes in her essay, the teachings of the church must not only articulate an historic identity but also must include the needs, concerns, and hopes of all persons, and particularly those who have been oppressed and at the margins of the church. This requires listening and insuring that all have voice in the process and the actual teachings of the church. What sometimes may appear as chaos and the loss of identity may in fact reflect what is most important to the identity and integrity of the Christian community.

The development of moral teachings on the part of the church is a matter of ecclesial polity or governance. The hope of the contributors to this volume is that this work may serve that task, especially in clarifying the purpose of moral teachings: "Who speaks for the church to whom on what? Why? And how?"

Endnotes

1. Paul Ramsey, *Who Speaks for the Church?* (Nashville: Abingdon, 1967).

2. James M. Gustafson, *Protestant and Roman Catholic Ethics* (Chicago: University of Chicago Press, 1978), p. 130.

3. Robert Hood's *Social Teachings in the Episcopal Church* (Harrisburg, PA: Morehouse Publishing, 1990) is the only other study that provides some such historical summary.

1

Decorum as Doctrine:
Teachings on Human Sexuality

Harmon L. Smith

"Human sexuality" is a protean phrase which nowadays covers an extraordinarily broad area of human affairs, and whose boundaries are far from fixed. It has been variously employed to address queries ranging from "why do we behave sexually?" to "how do we behave sexually?" to "how ought we behave sexually?" And in one context or another it has elicited comment on a long, but probably not yet exhaustive, list of topics.

Biological structures and functions of genitalia and reproductive systems and organs, abortion, celibacy, contraception, pornography, pedophilia, incest, sterilization, sexuality and aging, bestiality, genetic anomalies (such as the Triple-X, XXY, XO, and XYY syndromes), transvestism, autoeroticism, fetishism, transsexual surgery, oral-genital stimulation, necrophilia, voyeurism, exhibitionism, sadomasochism, sexual malfunction (e.g., impotence, premature ejaculation, frigidity, dyspareunia), brain and spinal cord injury sexuality, homosexuality, marriage, "enhancements" (the euphemism for breast augmentation, hip reduction, penile implant, *et al.*), new reproductive technologies (including artificial insemination, in vitro fertilization, and surrogacy), prenatal diagnostics, divorce, monogamy, polygamy, and remarriage—these topics indicate something of the breadth and depth which that list encompasses.

It is not unusual that active moralists turn to the church for endorsement of their causes—sometimes for political reasons, sometimes for the sake of sentimentality, and sometimes because conscience niggles when its sense of what is good and right does not enjoy the church's blessing. Blue Book reports of the Standing Commission on Human Affairs and Health and the proceedings of recently established diocesan commissions make it clear that many of these topics have been considered *in camera*. It is equally clear from the journals of General Convention that relatively few of them have surfaced on the floor for legislative consideration. Careful exegesis and extensive analysis would suggest far-reaching implications for teachings on human sexuality from resolutions which have, in fact, been adopted by Convention; but that task is beyond our borders here. Above all else that is signified by these observations, it is manifest that the occasion and ethos of General Convention is better suited to conducting other kinds of business than serious and sober promulgation of theological and ethical teachings.

For too long the lack of sustained and coherent theological reflection on the nature and meaning of human sexuality, and of Christian marriage in particular, has prevented the Episcopal Church from identifying crucial moral issues, providing teaching which enables engagement with and appropriation of Christian faith with regard to human sexuality, and informing and instructing the conscience of its communicants. In consequence, ECUSA—like most other contemporary mainline churches—has become captive to an agenda which is in principle largely not its own but is dictated by its environing culture.

Unsurprisingly, the Episcopal Church in the United States of America has not made official pronouncement on all, or even most, of these matters concerning human sexuality. The list of issues is long, sometimes scientifically complex, and understandably daunting; but beyond that, a large number of these matters received extensive (and many think, adequate) attention centuries ago, and others appear to be too recent for knowledgeable and discriminating ecclesial comment. Perhaps more to the point as expressive of the present state of ECUSA, and suggesting once more that fact may be stranger than fiction, even the presiding bishop has stated that General Convention is still in debate on the topic of sexuality and that "it is the mind of the House" that debate and dialogue be continued.

The 1988 General Convention confirmed that Joan Rivers' signature line "Can we talk?" is descriptively accurate of this church's current disposition. On the sixth day of Convention, a resolution was introduced that ECUSA adopt as its own a 1987 resolution of the General Synod of the Church of England which stated:

. . . that the biblical and traditional teaching on chastity and fidelity in personal relationships is a response to, and expression of, God's love for each one of us. . . .

1. that sexual intercourse is an act of total commitment which belongs properly within a permanent marriage relationship;

2. that fornication and adultery are sins against this ideal, and are to be met by a call to repentance and the exercise of compassion;

3. that homosexual genital acts also fall short of this ideal, and are likewise to be met by a call to repentance and the exercise of compassion;

4. that all Christians are called to be exemplary in all spheres of morality, including sexual morality, and that holiness of life is particularly required for Christian leaders.[1]

Following debate, the resolution reappeared on the eighth day in a substantively revised, and in comparison anemic, form as Report #83 of the Committee on Social and Urban Affairs. In this version, the preface to the four salient points, together with the fourth point, were incorporated into an introduction; points 1, 2, and 3 were omitted in their entirety; and three new "resolveds" were introduced. Following some debate and modest amendment, Resolution D120s was adopted. It provides:

1. that each diocese and congregation be strongly urged to provide opportunities for "open dialogue on human sexuality, in which we, as members of this church, both heterosexual and homosexual, may study, pray, listen to and share our convictions and concerns, our search for stable, loving, and committed relationships, and our journey toward wholeness and holiness";

2. that "Scripture, tradition, reason and experience, supplemented by the 1976, 1979, 1982, and 1985 statements from the General Convention on human sexuality, the resolution adopted by the General Synod of the Church of England in November, 1987, and the 1988 report of the Standing Commission on Human Affairs and Health, and ongoing scientific research be commended for use in this dialogue. . . ."

3. and that dioceses and congregations report to the

Standing Commission on Human Affairs and Health, who are to "evaluate the reports and produce a composite report for presentation to the 70th General Convention."[2]

Human sexuality issues were also prominent (and volatile!) at the 70th General Convention. Shortly before the Phoenix meeting convened in 1991, and despite a request from the presiding bishop that he refrain, the Rt. Rev. Ronald Haines, bishop of Washington, ordained an avowed lesbian to the priesthood. Bishop Browning had said that the ordination could "trigger the sort of attention that may make positive dialogue more difficult." Bishop Haines responded that, although his decision might be disappointing and upsetting, he was "not convinced that homosexuality in itself should be a bar to ordination in every case."[3]

Before Convention adjourned, a resolution to censure Bishop Haines (together with the former assisting bishop of Newark, the Rt. Rev. Walter Righter) was introduced in the House of Bishops by retired bishop Gerald McAllister (of Oklahoma). Bishop McAllister's motion was defeated; in its place the bishops adopted a resolution which recognized "the pain and damage to the collegiality and credibility of this house and to parts of the whole church when individual bishops and dioceses ordain sexually active gay and lesbian persons in the face of repeated statements of this House of Bishops and the General Convention against such ordinations."[4]

In preparation for the 70th General Convention, the Rt. Rev. William Frey, dean of Trinity Episcopal School for Ministry, introduced a proposed canon which would explicitly require clergy to abstain from sexual intercourse outside of Holy Matrimony. This resolution, even after revision and emendation, failed. In its place the delegates adopted yet another "compromise resolution," this one:

a) affirming the church's traditional teaching on marriage (namely, that "physical sexual expression is appropriate only within the life-long monogamous union of husband and wife"),

b) acknowledging "discontinuity" between the church's teaching and the experience of some of its members,

c) confessing the inability of our leaders to come to a definite conclusion on these matters, and

d) calling for continued study and a "pastoral teaching" by the bishops with contributions from grass roots clergy and laity.

While this is the latest statement from Convention, there have been other resolutions over the past four decades which speak more directly and materially to issues associated with human sexuality. Because they are sometimes confused, it may be useful to observe here that theological ethics and pastoral care are related but neither synonymous nor identical and that these resolutions are meant to display ECUSA's formal (and most think, official) moral teaching. They are, accordingly, exempla of ECUSA's theological ethics. And while pastoral care may moderate these teachings, it may not materially change them.

From 1949 to the present, three topics have emerged with a measure of prominence in ECUSA's resolutions: marriage, ordaining a homosexual person, and blessing same-sex unions. As it happens, these three topics are distinguishable but not separable; each one impinges in discrete, and sometimes subtle, ways on the other two. Beyond our reach here, each one also has a long and complex history which displays its own evolving identity together with its relationship(s) with presiding cultural practices and religious beliefs. It may appear somewhat arbitrary to choose one of them as a starting point; on the other hand, marriage comprises in many ways the penumbra concept under which much of the current discussion proceeds.

Teachings on Marriage

Marriage was not made a sacrament in the Western church until the Fourth Lateran Council in 1215. Prior to that time, marriage appears to have been largely defined by the legal contract and regarded as a family matter, to which the church might or might not add its blessing. The most articulate theologian on these matters, St. Augustine, had held that our sexual impulses are sinful because they not only distract us from God but also constitute the means by which we communicate Adamic/original sin to our progeny. This would appear to leave us in an awkward, if not intractable, difficulty with respect both to certain biblical mandates and the perpetuation of the race. Marriage alone could not be justified because it presupposed sexual intimacy. Augustine's contemporary, St. Jerome, concluded that the only good which could come from marriage was children who would themselves be celibate! But Augustine's fertile and pious imagination offered a creative and novel outlet: the procreation of children rescues, and even sanctifies, sexual intercourse, and the indissolubility of marriage provides a stable and nurturing context for the family.

When the Fourth Lateran Council made marriage a sacrament in the Western church, it did nothing to modify the basic elements of Augustinian theology. It is not surprising, then, that when "the causes for which matrimony was ordained" appeared in the 1549 Prayer Book, more than 300 years later, they followed in sequence the principal features which the church (either tacitly or explicitly) had embraced since the fourth century: marriage is licit for Christians for the procreation of children, as a remedy against sin, and for the mutual society, help, and comfort of each other.

In his monumental *Commentary on the American Prayer Book*, Marion Hatchett provided an astonishing historical perspective on the marriage rite. First he cites the exhortation of the 1549 Prayer Book, which contained the classical "causes for which matrimony was ordained":

One cause was the procreation of children, to be brought up in the fear and nurture of the Lord, and praise of God. Secondly, it was ordained for a remedy against sin, and to avoid fornication, that such persons as be married might live chastely in matrimony, and keep themselves undefiled members of Christ's body. Thirdly, for the mutual society, help, and comfort that the one ought to have of the other, both in prosperity and adversity. Into the which holy estate these two persons present come now to be joined.[5]

Then he observed that the section on the purposes of marriage was (inexplicably?) deleted, not only from the exhortation but entirely, in the first American Prayer Book of 1789.[6]

Trying to imagine how the traditional theological and liturgical reasons for including these purposes happened to be dismissed is not easy. The difficulty is only escalated when one tries also to imagine how the anthropological, economic, and sociological reasons for having large families in this new land could be so summarily and similarly disregarded. In a single omission, both Christian tradition and existential location were abandoned!

Any comment whatever on the purposes of marriage remained absent from American Prayer Books for 160 years, until 1949, when that feature from the 1549 Prayer Book was restored in a rephrased and reordered way by Canon I.17.3. When the 1949 Committee on Constitution and Canons recommended adoption of what we now know as the "Declaration of Intention" (Canon I.18.3[d]), it prefaced the resolution by declaring: "Certain additions and clarification *which do not deal with doctrine* seem desirable, and provisions should be made for further study of the matter."[7] That the declaration would "not deal with doctrine" belies both the substance of the resolution and its original intention. In its further revised form, the "Declaration of Intention" currently states:

> We, A.B. and C.D., desiring to receive the blessing of Holy Matrimony in the Church, do solemnly declare that we hold marriage to be a lifelong union of husband and wife as it is set forth in the *Book of Common Prayer.*
>
> We believe that the union of husband and wife, in heart, body, and mind, is intended by God for their mutual joy; for the help and comfort given one another in prosperity and adversity; and, when it is God's will, for the procreation of children and their nurture in the knowledge and love of the Lord.
>
> And we do engage ourselves, so far as in us lies, to make our utmost effort to establish this relationship and to seek God's help thereto.

The entire second paragraph of this declaration is incorporated into the exhortation which introduces the marriage rite in the 1979 *Book of Common Prayer.*[8] The first paragraph of the declaration makes it plain that Holy Matrimony is a joining of man and woman; there is no mention anywhere in the exhortation of marriage as a "lifelong union of husband and wife." That intention of indissolubility does occur, however, as the final element in the consents, which are exchanged immediately following the exhortation.

A further question arises when the Prayer Book does not explain, nor is it otherwise made clear in rubrics or canons, why the only prayer among those in the 1979 marriage rite which is specifically marked as "may be omitted" is the one which speaks of procreation: "Bestow on them, if it is your will, the gift and heritage of children, and the grace to bring them up to know you, to love you, and to serve you." Whether to include this prayer seems to be an enigmatic, if not in some respects an anomalous, choice. On the face of it, the rubric

appears to make the procreation of children optional according to a couple's preference; but both the marriage canon and
the exhortation appear to leave the matter of having or not
having the blessing of children dependent upon God's will.
What has changed, of course, and what requires our sympa-
thetic attention and critical reflection, is the means by which
we understand and respond to God's will. In this case, we
appear to have moved from identification of God's will with
the (natural) biological process of reproduction to human dis-
cernment and private choice. Some believe that such a circumstance represents our confusion about the respective roles
of human and divine authority; others will think that this is a
muddle more broadly about the purposes of human sexuality
and the place of human interventions in biological processes;
and still others will claim that it merely reflects this church's
commitment to a *via media*. All are probably correct.[9] What
appears to be indisputably clear is that here is yet another
example of making important changes which reflect different
theological understandings *without* ever identifying those
diverse (and probably dissonant) understandings.

In the proceedings of this 1949 Convention, there is no
account of why the explicit intention of the House of Bishops
Committee, which meant to have the church's doctrine agreed
to and accepted by prospective marriage partners, was explicitly altered to the converse position when the Committee on
Constitution and Canons recommended adoption of the
canon. That is a serious move which preserved the form, but
not the substance, of the church's teaching and doctrine. One
is left to wonder just how it might be that the acknowledged
purposes of marriage could ignore, or fail to deal directly
with, the church's doctrine of Holy Matrimony.[10]

While certain features of this church's understanding of
Christian marriage are clear from the canons and the marriage
rite, there are others which are confusing if not patently confused. It is clear, for example, that we believe that marriage is
heterosexual, monogamous, consensual, covenanted within
the community of faith, with the intent to be lifelong, and to
be entered into advisedly and deliberately. And it is clear that
the *Book of Common Prayer's* understanding of the unitive
and procreative purposes of marriage permits no unprincipled
separation of these two. It is also clear that this church
requires that both parties be marriageable according to the
laws of the state, and that at least one of them be baptized.

Considering the broad range views among its clergy, it is not clear that ECUSA believes marriage to be a sacrament, a sign of God's grace in the world. Nor is it clear why we have reordered the purposes of marriage, subordinating the purpose of procreation to the purpose of mutual joy, or whether God or the couple will determine that their marriage is to be blessed by children, or why it is sufficient that only one of the parties be baptized. Reflecting the ambivalence in this church about whether marriage is a sacrament, it is also unclear, both to the church which blesses and to the couple seeking its blessing, what it means precisely that the church "blesses" this union; especially if, as many believe, the couple marry themselves before priest and people, who only witness the event. In sum, it is not clear who is in charge of the meaning and purpose of Christian marriage—the church or the couple—and this, in turn, raises a number of questions about whether the modifier "Christian" controls the meaning and purpose of marriage, or whether "Christian" functions as a gloss, a dispensable adjunct, to what are fundamentally secular or pagan or legal understandings.

There is probably broad agreement that each age must recast, and possibly rewrite, a theology of marriage in order to connect its time with the meaning of the marriage covenant to which Christ himself witnessed in his own time.[11] And that process may well be what these rephrasings and reorderings in our rites and canons are about. But ECUSA has tended to approach this task unsystematically, and as a result *ad hoc* revisions and resolutions have invited lacunae, inconsistencies, and (quite literally) contradictions. Such an outcome in itself is not surprising, as anyone familiar with archaisms in the civil and criminal statutory law knows. It happens because zeal for a particular piece of legislation exceeds commitment to cogency and coherence in the positive law. All the same, the long-term price for this enthusiasm may be larger than its immediate benefits. With the statutory law, people innocent of any part in its revision are obliged to pay for clarity and definition through costly litigation. With canon law, and particularly as it is adjudicated in this church, the costs may be greater because they will entail not only money, but trust, commitment, and faith.

So a number of obvious questions occur about ECUSA's teachings on marriage. For a direct example we might ask: do we as a church still believe what Augustine taught with respect to these matters? Answers may seem equally obvious: to this direct question, for example, experience suggests that plainly we do not. And if we do not believe what Augustine taught, what, if anything, do we offer in its place?

As it happens, we do in fact continue to share some of the same language, even some of the same conceptual apparatus, with Augustine, but they do not seem to bear the same freighted meanings. Here is a wonderful illustration of what Alasdair MacIntryre has called "simulacra of morality," a situation marked by possession of bits and pieces of what were once cogent and coherent conceptual schemes, but which are used now as fragments lacking those contexts from which their significance derived.[12] Still, as the puzzling juxtaposition of the current marriage canon, exhortation, and prayers suggests, not believing these things apparently does not mean abandoning them. We often retain a form of the church's historical teaching which is more recognizable than its substance.

Ordaining a Homosexual Person
ECUSA's lack of a cogent and coherent theology of Christian marriage, and of human sexuality more generally, has plainly taxed its tortured (and sometimes turgid) utterances on homosexuality. Following a resolution by the 65th General Convention in 1976, which stated that "homosexual persons are children of God who have a full and equal claim with all other persons upon the love, acceptance, and pastoral concern and care of the Church," and in response to a mandate "to study in depth the matter of the ordination of homosexual persons and report its findings, along with recommendations . . . to the next General Convention," the first report of the newly constituted Standing Commission on Human Affairs and Health,[13] given in 1979, contained a lengthy statement on human sexuality, together with a proposed resolution. The chair's introduction to the statement began with the descriptively accurate demurrer that this is not "a polished and definitive study but . . . a background paper on an intricate and sensitive subject."[14] Similarly, the proposed resolution reflected the commission's inability to get directly and precisely to a point of definite consequence,[15] although it did form the basis for the final form of the resolution which was adopted.

Omitting the several "whereas" clauses, the meat of that 1979 resolution read as follows:

Resolved, the House of Deputies concurring, That this General Convention recommend to Bishops, Pastors, Vestries, Commissions on Ministry and Standing Committees, the following considerations as they continue to exercise their proper canonical functions in the selection and approval of persons for ordination:

1. There are many human conditions, some of them in the area of sexuality, which bear upon a person's suitability for ordination;

2. Every ordinand is expected to lead a life which is 'a wholesome example to all people' (*Book of Common Prayer*, pp. 517, 532, 544). There should be no barrier to the ordination of qualified persons of either heterosexual or homosexual orientation whose behavior the Church considers wholesome;

3. We re-affirm the traditional teaching of the Church on marriage, marital fidelity and sexual chastity as the standard of Christian sexual morality. Candidates for ordination are expected to conform to this standard. Therefore, we believe it is not appropriate for this Church to ordain a practicing homosexual, or any person who is engaged in heterosexual relations outside of marriage."[16]

In response to this action by Convention, twenty-one bishops gave notice in a signed statement that they would not accept or implement these recommendations in their dioceses. That recusancy notwithstanding, however, this resolution remains the official position of ECUSA.[17] Although the resolution explicitly rejects "barrier(s) to the ordination of qualified persons of either heterosexual or homosexual orientation," it imposes restraints on the expression and practice of that orientation.

The limiting clause, which asserts that "it is not appropriate for this Church to ordain a practicing homosexual, or any person who is engaged in heterosexual relations outside of marriage," identifies two disqualifying standards. It also provokes much of the friction, if not enmity, which now marks discussions of human sexuality in this church. In the succeeding twelve years the situation is not much changed, as both the acrimonious debate and the resolutions which were adopted at the 1991 General Convention attest. The internal logic of the 1979 resolution, however, is consistent: human sexual intercourse is restricted to marriage, and marriage is restricted to couples which are composed of one man and one woman.

Integrity is the national organization of lesbians and gay men in the Episcopal Church. On 3 July 1989, at its convention in San Francisco, the delegates adopted a number of resolutions which addressed the role and function of ECUSA communicants who are also homosexual. Two of these are directly pertinent to the matters treated in the 1979 General Convention resolution. In order to convey the full force of the discordance between them and the positions adopted by the 1979 General Convention, the Integrity resolutions need to be quoted in their entirety (again excepting the "whereas" prefaces):

> *Therefore be it resolved* that this 15th Anniversary Convention of Integrity calls upon the Standing Liturgical Commission of the Episcopal Church to prepare appropriate rites to restore to Lesbians and Gay men the ancient practice of sacramentally legitimizing our unions, and upon the 70th General Convention to approve the same and the Episcopal Church to press the state for full legal recognition of such same sex covenants of union.

> *Therefore be it resolved* that this 15th Anniversary Convention of Integrity calls upon the 70th General Convention of the Episcopal Church to amend the Canons of this Church to officially guarantee full and equal access to all rites, sacraments, and employment in the Church without regard to race, color, ethnic origin, sex, sexual orientation, physical disabilities, or age.[18]

The present bishop of Newark was not among those dissenting signatories to the 1979 statement; but ten years later, in a letter to members of the House of Bishops dated 8 December 1989, the Rt. Rev. John S. Spong announced that he would ordain "a gay male who lives in a committed relationship with his partner." It was clear to those familiar with Bishop Spong's recent writings that this was a considered move, underwritten by the positions he had affirmed in various essays and perhaps especially in one of his latest books.[19] With the recent history of irregular ordinations in this church, Bishop Spong's unilateral action also appeared closely to parallel the Philadelphia ordinations of ECUSA's first women priests.

Included with his letter were two papers: one by the bishop entitled "Why I ordained a non-celibate gay male to the priesthood," and the other an account by the ordinand of "his journey into the priesthood." Robert Williams' ordination on 16 December 1989 was widely noted in both religious and secular news media and although the bishop contended that the 1979 resolution was advisory only and not binding, his action elicited perplexity and strong objection both within and without the church.

Barely a month later, in remarks before an Episcopal symposium on homosexual marriage, Williams declared that celibacy is unnatural and spiritually inhibiting, and that, as for monogamy, "It is crazy to hold up this ideal and pretend it's what we're doing, and we're not." He was also reported to have said, "If you're asking me do I think Mother Teresa ought to get laid, my answer is 'yes'."[20] Bishop Spong promptly reprimanded Williams and requested his resignation as director of The Oasis, a diocesan ministry to homosexuals. The priest was not asked to renounce his ordination. The executive council of the Episcopal Synod of America, however, passed a resolution asking the bishop to resign and promising to work to bring charges against him in the House of Bishops if he declined to do so.

On 20 February 1990 the presiding bishop, together with the members of his Council of Advice, issued a statement in which they affirmed the position taken in the 1979 resolution, disassociated themselves from the action of the Standing Committee and the Bishop of Newark in carrying out this ordination, and disapproved unilateral actions by bishops, dioceses, or parishes which do not adhere to the actions of General Convention. The House of Bishops, meeting in Washington, D.C., on 18 September 1990, voted 78–74 to "disassociate" itself from Bishop Spong's ordination of Robert Williams, and to "affirm and support" the February statement, which acknowledged that it is this church's position that it is "inappropriate" to ordain practicing homosexual persons.[21]

Given the language of the 1979 resolution, it may be arguable that the resolution does not have binding power. That General Convention did no more than "recommend" consideration of these qualifications for ordination, which were known at the time to be volatile and robust, might allow one to interpret the resolution as "advisory." Moreover, it does not stretch credibility with respect to such important matters as

these—and irrespective of their potential for dispute and dissension—to say that merely to "recommend" is an anemic
commendation.

All the same, what is at stake here is not linguistics or
word-games, or a contest of imagination which pits the clever
against the clod. What is at stake is the unity of the church
and the determination of its constituent communicants to preserve order and fellowship. Overall, and regrettably, this is not
an isolated political claim for autonomy within the parishes
and dioceses, and among the priests and bishops, of this
church. Those familiar with ECUSA's recent history will recognize this episode as only the latest in a series of moves
which challenge the coherence of its polity. The arguments
share a remarkable similarity to the ones advanced following
the Philadelphia ordinations in that they appeal to the letter of
the resolution and not to its spirit. At the end of the day, the
fault lies with both the bishops and the General Convention,
and it would be self-serving for either to lay their blame at the
other's feet. It remains to be seen whether a General
Convention will make it clear beyond reasonable doubt
whether the 1979 resolution is advisory or binding.

At the Phoenix Convention in 1991, the House of Bishops
declined to censure two bishops who had ordained avowed
and practicing homosexuals to the priesthood. And the so-
called compromise resolution which was adopted appears to
say that, while ECUSA affirms the church's traditional teaching on marriage, its leaders are unable to come to a definitive
conclusion about these matters. Because there is "discontinuity" between the church's acknowledged teaching and the
experience of some of its members, it therefore should continue to study these matters while bishops (with input from
both clergy and laity) offer "pastoral teaching!" Depending on
hermeneutic, this can be read as (among other things) ambiguity, confusion, irony, equivocation, or just plain contradiction.

Or consider: what can it mean, as in the 1979 resolution,
to say that this church affirms homosexual persons but disapproves homosexual behavior? Actually, ECUSA has not said
precisely that. What it has said is:

> Homosexual persons are children of God who have a
> full and equal claim with all other persons upon the
> love, acceptance, and pastoral concerns of the church.
> *The Journal of the General Convention*, 1976, p. A–69
> This General Convention expresses its conviction that

homosexual persons are entitled to equal protection of the law with all other citizens, and calls upon our society to see that such protection is provided in actuality.

The Journal of the General Convention, 1976, p. A–17; reaffirmed in 1982, *The Journal of the General Convention*, 1982, p. D–61a

We affirm the traditional teaching of the Church on marriage, marital fidelity, and sexual chastity as the standard of Christian morality. Candidates for ordination are expected to conform to this standard. Therefore, we believe it is not appropriate for this Church to ordain a practicing homosexual, or any person who is engaged in heterosexual relations outside of marriage.

The Journal of the General Convention, 1979, p. A–535

The 68th General Convention urge each diocese of this Church to find an effective way to foster a better understanding of homosexual persons, to dispel myths and prejudices about homosexuality, to provide pastoral support, and to give life to the claim of homosexual persons 'upon the love, acceptance, and pastoral care and concern of the Church' as recognized by the General Convention resolution of 1976.

The Journal of the General Convention, 1985, p. D–082s

Taken together, and as a whole, these statements materially (1) affirm and support homosexual persons as such, endorse guaranty of their civil rights, and offer them "the love, acceptance, and pastoral care and concern of the Church"; and (2) withhold ordination in this church from persons who engage in homosexual practices, as well as from persons who engage in heterosexual intercourse outside of marriage. The ambivalence reflected in these statements betrays ECUSA's double-mindedness and indicates that ECUSA is deeply suspicious of the moral legitimacy of homosexuality in the context of Christian faith and life. Its piecemeal affirmation and fractional denial only confirm that this is so. So while these statements do not say it precisely, they do seem tantamount to saying that this church loves and accepts homosexual persons but views homosexual practices as morally inappropriate if not opprobrious.

Is it little wonder that all of us, homosexuals and hetero-sexuals alike, should be confused? And can there be little astonishment that homosexuals should wonder how they can be simultaneously loved for who they are but morally suspect for what they do? A comparable exercise in symbolic logic would reveal the inconsistency, and the frank hypocrisy, of this attempt by ECUSA (together with other mainline reformed churches) to have it both ways, to be everything to everybody. Behavior cannot be abstracted from the person whose behavior it is. For sentimental reasons we may suppose that we can separate liars from lying, or patriots from fierce defense of country, or homosexual persons from homosexual practices, but that is a compound mistake inasmuch as we both deceive ourselves about what is really going on here, and invite the object of our sentimentality to a fragmented and conflicted (which is fundamentally a dishonest) identity and existence. Christians, of all people, should know better. Character and conduct, belief and behavior, affirmation and action—these belong together for personal and moral whole-ness. Over the long haul, we would do better to keep silent until we can confidently speak with a larger measure of clarity and precision, and in continuity with scripture, tradition, and cognate teachings.

The case for "loving the sinner but hating the sin" is inherited from a liberalism which was not overburdened with convictions, and it is, at best, problematic, unless we are com-fortable, as most of us are not, with a bifurcated and schizo-phrenic moral psychology. The greater weight of the evidence—historical, legal, social, moral, religious, and other-wise—is, in fact, on the side of wholeness and unity and integrity of the organism, which makes sense when the goal of education, preaching, medicine, law, and other human inter-ventions in the way things would be "naturally" without them is to train their target clientele to certain self-understandings, on the assumption that the right character will tend to engen-der the right behavior.

Although there is little question that "being" and "doing" are reciprocally influential in moral formation, Western phi-losophy from Plato onwards has generally assigned a synergis-tic priority to "being." So while we certainly hold people praise- or blameworthy for what they do, for how they act and behave, we also take their self-understanding into account when we assign accountability. That is why we excuse children and the mentally disadvantaged from some behaviors for which we punish putatively mature adults. Beyond that, however, "hypocrisy" is an odious word in both secular and religious circles. Sometimes as bad as the action itself is the violated trust, the stark mendacity, which the action signifies. The church, like other cultural institutions, is a school for character. And the church, like other cultural institutions, has its particular vision of the character which it means to school. In the Anglican tradition, this vision is formed by both special revelation and the natural moral law. Jeremy Taylor, for example, could argue Jesus' command to love God, neighbor, and self as correspondent to and commensurate with both God's nature and human nature, and thus to the natural moral law. ECUSA should be careful that it is its particular vision, and not another, which it undertakes to embody and communicate.

Blessing Same-sex Unions

If the 1979 resolution is advisory only, as Bishop Spong claimed, it might be supposed that the logic which underwrote his ordination of a non-celibate gay male to the priesthood would also underwrite the blessing of same-sex unions. But that would stretch credibility too far. The twenty-one bishops who dissented from that resolution acknowledged nonetheless that ECUSA holds same-sex unions to be illicit.[22]

Similarly, when the resolutions adopted at the Integrity convention in July 1989 call upon the upcoming 70th General Convention (1991) to "prepare appropriate rites to restore to Lesbians and Gay men the ancient practice of sacramentally legitimizing our unions" and "to press the state for full legal recognition of such same sex covenants of union," it is reasonable to conclude that Integrity acknowledges that the teaching of ECUSA is opposed to blessing same-sex unions.[23]

More precisely, Canon I.18.3, "Of the Solemnization of Holy Matrimony," would appear to make it quite clear in at least three places that only heterosexual unions are authorized: the parties must have the right "to contract a marriage according to the laws of the State" (I.18.2[a]); both parties shall "understand that Holy Matrimony is a physical and spiritual union of a man and woman" (I.18.2[b]); and both parties shall sign a declaration which includes the solemn profession that "[we] hold marriage to be a lifelong union of husband and wife" (I.18.3[d]).

That ECUSA now prohibits blessing same-sex unions is indisputable from the evidence of several General Conventions and from the contents of its Prayer Book and canons. Nevertheless, *why* ECUSA has such a prohibition is less than clear. If its theology of human sexuality provided a lucid and compelling honoring of celibacy as a vocation to which some are called, it might appeal to that teaching—not in order to impose it as a lifestyle but in order to affirm its virtue as a vocation for some. If its theology of marriage included those classical Catholic arguments regarding procreation as the human analogue of God's characteristic generativity, it would be better positioned to deny its blessing to homosexual unions. Lacking a mandate that marriage embrace the blessing of children, one might look for a theology of marriage which is rooted in natural law and nominates heterosexuality as typical and normative, and homosexuality as abnormal and aberrant. There are surely indications that such a natural law theory underlies much of the church's understanding of human sexuality; but these are too often only indications, and not the kind of sustained and systematic argument which makes a coherent and compelling claim.

Can ECUSA Be a Teaching Church?

We have suggested that ECUSA's teaching about the ordination and marriage of homosexual persons, and its theology of marriage, are in disarray. In part, we can account for this relatively erratic and disordered circumstance by acknowledging the church-state connection, which has alternately puzzled and pleased the church since the times of Constantine and Justinian. At the end of the twentieth century, nobody ought to doubt that there are inherent risks in relationships between a confessional religious body and its political environment. Our forebears in both England and this country probably appreciated that fact better than we have done in recent years, trying as they did to steer a course between the Scylla of church co-optation and the Charybdis of sectarian separation.

Our tendency has been to underestimate the actual as well as potential conflicts between piety and citizenship as these impinge upon matters associated with human sexuality. We have done that, in part, because we have not always reckoned the difference it ought to make that we are a particular kind of religious people and not merely a special-interest group within the general population. There is a difference between being responsive to issues which arise for crisis-intervention from without, and having our agenda for holy living composed for us by extra-ecclesial groups and interests. And there is a truly significant difference between the civil rights of persons, which vary enormously from one political realm to another, and the image of God, which does not vary from culture to culture and which has a prior claim upon our moral life.

The documentary evidence suggests that when we have failed to appreciate these and kindred differences, our pronouncements have been rather more reflexive than reflective. At its best, the church should self-consciously reserve the right to speak only to matters which are plainly within its ken and its authority. In introductory biology classes, students are shown how increasing electrical stimulation of the sciatic nerve of a frog produces incremental twitching of the frog's leg until the stimulation achieves an intensity to which the nerve is no longer able to respond. When that happens, the leg goes limp despite maintenance of the electrical charge; biologists call that "biological overload." Something similar happens when an ecclesial legislative body attempts to be responsive to the total range of stimuli applied to it: the stimulus current is intensely charged, but the organ becomes flaccid as a function of legislative overload.

How to be a community of Christian believers, who take with utter seriousness God's incarnation as Jesus in a world of many competing ideologies, has not always been a prominent, to say nothing of controlling, question for us. Institutional wholeness, cooperation in the name of comprehensiveness, response to the irrepressible lobbying of a special-interest group—these and other influences appear too often to have directed both the initiative for and the formulation of this church's resolutions on urgent moral issues. In this respect, ECUSA can claim the company of all the mainline Protestant churches.[24]

Even so, in the matter of human sexuality, these conflicts are limited. So, for example, ECUSA has no conflict in its citizenship duties with respect to homosexuality, nor are there any apparent conflicts in the matter of ordaining homosexual persons, because neither of these matters is addressed by statute. All the same, a potential problem does arise with blessing same-sex unions when homosexual marriage is not permitted by law. Here is an issue which ECUSA must face squarely; but on its own theological terms, and not those of Anglo-American jurisprudence.

"Getting out of the marrying business," as some have suggested ECUSA ought to do, would not solve this problem. Only an understanding of the relationship between church and state clearly different from the one we have now will resolve this tension. Recent litigation, frequently involving medical care, shows that there is little reason to expect that the guarantees of religious freedom in this country will extend to religious practices which are unacceptable before the law. The purpose of the statutory law is to guard and protect the common good, and the fact that religious belief cannot be freely acted out ought to be appreciated by religious people for the restricted right that it is. That the law intervenes in these ways is probably unavoidable as long as "religion" is defined so broadly as to include virtually anything that wants to call itself by that name. Religious liberty on these terms is a shibboleth; it has a hollow ring to it.

There is more than enough evidence to make compelling the claim that it is naive to expect uniformity in any group, even when only two or three are gathered together in the name of Jesus, or marriage, or General Convention. So we ought to expect that there will be protagonists and antagonists in the church; indeed, we ought to welcome and celebrate the spiritual and intellectual abrasion which they generate, even though we cannot say prospectively how much diversity in these areas we can (or in fact ought to) encourage. But we cannot do that in the name of mere tolerance, by making room for various, even disparate, points of view. We can only celebrate that kind of controversy when there are substantial and shared reference points which keep us honest about the real stakes of the argument, and in relation to which the pros and cons can be taken seriously.

Meanwhile, virtually everybody in our individualist and autonomous culture will be offended by some particular ecclesial teaching. To say, as for example about homosexuality, that we will not divide the church over this issue shows both compassion toward different constituencies and the desire for an institutional equivalent of the "get-out-of-jail-free" card. At issue, of course, is whether congregations, clergy, and bishops will take seriously the church's pronouncements. Beyond that is our apparent uncertainty about how we may responsibly take account of dissent within the church. At the moment, we seem to have a paucity of resources for dealing constructively with dissent; but scarcity is not a void, and there are some assets on which we can draw.

So, while we do not need to suppose that our teachings on human sexuality are definitive, we do need to know that they are definite (insofar as within us lies). Beyond that, we need to know that they are somehow contiguous with our inheritance, the gift of scripture and tradition and reason. Believing that what we teach about marriage, or the ordination of homosexual persons to the church's ministry, or the blessing of same-sex unions is as clear-cut and lucid as we can state it, and as faithful as we know how to connect it to the *sensus communis* of the *corpus mysticum*, is no more than our bounden duty and service.

Outwardly, of course, Christian marriages appear to be indistinguishable from pagan ones; objectively, both we and they seem to be engaged in many of the same actions. But there is a difference, which is an internal one of will and intention. It may have been that particular difference which our Lord had in mind when he defined adultery as a matter of the heart (Mt. 5:27–28) and invited those "who are without sin" to stone the adulteress (Jn. 8:3–11). It is clearly a difference which we have long recognized by providing a number of nouns to identify specific acts of human sexual congress: rape, incest, conjugal love, adultery, pedophilia. These words help us to understand that the meaning and purpose of an action is not self-evident in the action itself, and that we need interpretive clues from the actors if we are to perceive correctly what is going on here. And that, in turn, suggests that actors themselves need to know where they can turn to find out which actions are good, right, and true—and why. The church rightly claims the role as referent for these questions when they mean to ask what difference it makes that these relationships and actions are modified by "Christian."

So, for example, as regards the purposes of marriage, the church ought to say plainly that having children is a vocation for Christians; that we neither choose to have children nor have them because we cannot avoid it; that having children is a duty for Christians because we believe that we are commanded to do so as an expression of our determination to witness faithfully to the God of Abraham and Sarah, Isaac and Rebekah, Jacob and Leah, Joseph and Mary, Jesus, and Paul, and to live in this selfish and sinful world by the power of the world to come. That kind of forthright rhetoric will doubtless prompt some to observe that there is a difference between being a fool for Christ's sake and a damned fool, and the force of that crude observation deserves the church's attention. So we can add that this does not mean, of course, that there is no place for celibacy as a vocation and that all Christians must have children, or that "having children" may not be accomplished by adoption or some other alternative to "natural" conception, gestation, and parturition, or that virginity, as Luther said, is an evasion of social responsibility. And we can further acknowledge that these matters are better served by casuistry and pastoral care than legislation.

But ECUSA has typically forfeited its claims to be a "teaching" church, and it has preferred to delegate controversial opinion giving to individual communicants while aligning its official position(s) with "the inherent comprehensiveness of the church." Why is this? Why are we not a teaching church? Answers are legion, and a sample of those suggested to me include:

- we have nothing to teach;
- we fear encroaching on the autonomy of individuals to decide these matters for themselves;
- we believe that the gospel is not gift, but discovery;
- we equate instruction with indoctrination, and indoctrination is inappropriate;
- the church is one among many value-affirming institutions and communities, and none has a corner on the truth;
- we have failed to understand the office of bishop in this church;
- we understand our ecclesial life as chiefly or solely diocesan or parochial;
- bishops and other clergy are principally managers and therapists;
- the laity does not want to be party to a teaching church;
- ECUSA has no magisterium.

What would we need to do to become a teaching church? At the outset, we would need to reverse and/or recast all of the above.

It is not popular nowadays to say some of these things, and some think it perverse to venture them on behalf of the church. On the other hand, we know that a pagan and secular environment has eroded many of the traditionally authentic ways of understanding and intending ourselves as disciples of Jesus Christ; and that this development threatens not only the piety of individual Christians, but the legitimacy of institutionalized Christian communities as well. In that respect, our time may not be fundamentally different from other times in the opportunity which it offers ECUSA and other Christian churches for obedient and faithful discipleship, and in the occasion it provides for reliance wholly on the grace of our Lord Jesus Christ, the love of God, and the fellowship of the Holy Spirit.

I want to acknowledge my great appreciation to Mrs. Carol Cummings and Professor David Scott of Virginia Theological Seminary, and to Ms. Michelle Francis, the Archivist of the Diocese of North Carolina, for their valuable assistance with bibliographic searches and acquisitions related to the preparation of this essay.

Endnotes

1. *Journal of the General Convention*, 1988, p. 183.

2. Ibid., pp. 296–297.

3. Among many accounts of this episode and related events in both the religious and secular media, direct quotations here are taken from reports in *The Living Church* (5 January 1992), p. 8.

4. Quoted from an Episcopal News Service dispatch in the Diocese of North Carolina's *The Communicant* (September 1991), p. 6.

5. Marion J. Hatchett, *Commentary on the American Prayer Book* (New York: Seabury, 1981), p. 432. The traditional ends of Christian marriage, according to St. Augustine, are *bonum proles, bonum fides,* and *bonum sacramentum*; and the classical requirements for a valid marriage are *ratum et consummatum* (consent and consummation). See Edward Lambe Parsons and Bayard Hale Jones, *The American Prayer Book—Its Origins and Principles* (New York: Charles Scribner's Sons, 1937), p. 251.

6. Ibid., pp. 432–433.

7. *Journal of the General Convention*, 1949, p. 166. Underscoring mine.

8. See pp. 432–433. See also the *Journal of the General Convention*, 1988, pp. 702–703.

9. This new canon actually had its genesis in a special committee on "marriage legislation" of the House of Bishops, whose mandate included recommending to Convention any needed amendments to the canons on Holy Matrimony. Three years earlier, the House of Bishops had adopted, but the House of Deputies had rejected, a similar proposal; so now, in its report, the special committee prefaced its proposal for a declaration of intention with the following paragraph:

> A number of Bishops have suggested that *the statement of agreement with and acceptance of the Church's doctrine of Holy Matrimony* to be signed by the parties to a marriage, which was recommended by resolution of the last Convention, now be made a part of the Canon itself. This seems wise to your Committee both because the Lambeth Committee on pages 99 and 100 of its report recommends the signing of such a declaration, and *because its use opens the door to systematic discussion and instruction of brides and grooms.* (Ibid., p. 438. Underscoring mine.)

10. Of course, this is not the first (and plainly not the only) occasion when Convention has operated with this kind of doublespeak, which is defended in the name of "openness" and "comprehensiveness." A joint commission was charged to report to the 1916 Convention on the advisability of "revision and enrichment of the Prayer Book," with the stipulation "that no proposition involving the Faith and Doctrine of the Church shall be considered or reported upon by the Commission." [Cf. Thaddaeus A. Schnitker, *The Church's Worship: the 1979 American Book of Common Prayer in a Historical Perspective* (European University Studies: Series 23, Theology; Volume 351, Frankfurt am Main: Peter Lang, 1989), p. 98.] But, of course, changes affecting doctrine were made in the 1929 Prayer Book; not the least of which were collects for the departed, together with a petition for the departed in the "Prayer for the Whole State of Christ's Church." A detailed contemporary account of this phase of the production of the 1929 Prayer Book observed that both the commission and the Convention were

> wisely interpreting the 'Faith and Doctrine of the Church' as referring to the permissible bounds of

Anglican orthodoxy, and consequently exploring and developing our inherited liberties in every direction— *to the great enlargement of the inherent comprehensiveness of the Church.* (Parsons and Jones, pp. 59-60. Underscoring mine.)

11. Cf. Urban T. Holmes, "Six Theses on the Theology of Marriage," *St. Luke's Journal of Theology,* Vol. 27 (June 1984) 3:pp. 167 ff.

12. Alasdair MacIntryre, *After Virtue* (Notre Dame: University of Notre Dame Press, 1981), p. 2.

13. This commission was created at the 65th General Convention (1976) by combining two existing bodies, the Committee on Religion and Health and the Commission on the Church in Human Affairs. Cf. Canon I.1.2(g).

14. *The Blue Book: Reports of the Committees, Commissions, Boards, and Agencies of the General Convention of the Episcopal Church,* 1979, p. 69.

15. Ibid., p. 68.

16. *Journal of the General Convention of the Protestant Episcopal Church in the United States of America—Otherwise Known as the Episcopal Church* (The General Convention, Episcopal Church Center, 815 Second Avenue, New York, NY 10017), 1979, pp. C-88–89.

17. Ibid., pp. B-110–112.

18. While this is not the place to examine thoroughly the claim that ECUSA should "restore to Lesbians and Gay men the ancient practice of sacramentally legitimizing our unions," I want to note that this assertion is not self-evident and, in fact, misrepresents ecclesiastical history.

19. John S. Spong, *Living in Sin? A Bishop Rethinks Humans Sexuality* (Nashville: Abingdon, 1988).

20. *The Living Church* (18 February 1990), pp. 6–7; *Newsweek* (12 February 1990), p. 61.

21. *The Living Church* (14 October 1990), pp. 8, 15.

22. *Journal of the General Convention,* 1979, p. B-111.

23. This point is explicitly confirmed in a recent lengthy essay by Robert Williams, "Toward a Theology for Lesbian and Gay Marriage," (*Anglican Theological Review,* Vol. 72(1990) 2:pp. 134–157). Williams' thesis is "that a covenanted relationship between two women or two men is

just as much a Christian *marriage* as that between a man and a woman." (p. 135) Following the essay are five commentaries which wrestle, each in its own way, with whether the church which blesses, or the couple asking for its blessing, presides over the meaning(s) and purpose(s) of "Christian marriage."

24. Implementation of resolutions reflects similar commitments. For example, "Sexuality: A Divine Gift" was produced by a Task Force on Human Sexuality and Family Life Education, appointed by The Executive Council's Education for Mission and Ministry Unit in response to Resolution D-76a (1982), which mandated development of "educational ways by which the Church can assist its people . . . to develop moral and spiritual perspectives in matters relating to sexuality and family life." Conspicuously absent from the task force are any of the church's systematic, moral, pastoral, biblical, or historical theologians. Substantively, "Sexuality: A Divine Gift" either ignores what the church has taught, or subordinates the church's teaching to individual experience and discovery; and overall it reflects an absence of articulate doctrine together with a corresponding loss of theological skills. The roles allocated to God and church by this document are as supporting players to the main character of self; and the methodology is a frank inversion of I John 4:10 (i.e., this document claims that it is in and through our sexuality that we discover God's love). This resource is a wonderful example of much that is wrong with our overall approach to a theology of human sexuality, which fails to be historically literate, scripturally faithful, and continuous with tradition; but there is neither time nor space here to develop that criticism fully. Happily, this church has resources other than "Sexuality: A Divine Gift"; see, for example, "Sexuality and New Life," in David H. Smith, *Health and Medicine in the Anglican Tradition* (New York: Crossroad, 1986), pp. 69–96; and Philip Turner's *Sex, Money and Power* (Cambridge: Cowley Publications, 1985), esp. pp. 29–70.

2

New Technologies for
Assisted Reproduction

David H. Smith
Judith A. Granbois

New technologies for assisted reproduction fascinate and
frighten us; they offer hope and heartache; they challenge fundamental and long-standing values. The Episcopal Church has
attended recurrently to the moral questions raised by the new
technologies over the past twenty years. We want to report on
what the denomination has done and said and to make some
observations about the adequacy of these statements and about
the problems of authority and teaching responsibility.

Developing Teachings

Of the various relevant technologies,[1] the Episcopal
Church has focused primarily on in vitro fertilization (IVF),
surrogate motherhood, and artificial insemination (AI).
(Technically, AIH is artificial insemination using the husband's sperm; AID uses sperm from a donor.) In general, the
church has approved IVF and AIH; it has opposed surrogacy
and AID. Thus it has sanctioned technological assistance for
couples who are using their own gametes (sperm and ova), but
it has frowned upon if not condemned the introduction of a
third person into the reproductive relationship.[2]

One argument for this conclusion is based on the assertion
that technology and the use of prostheses are not in themselves wrong solely because they may be in some sense
"unnatural." For example, the 1970 report of the Joint
Commission on the Church in Human Affairs treats acquisi-
tion of knowledge positively, stressing the human role in creation, and supporting AIH.

[W]e believe that employment of artificial insemination by husband and wife is morally licit and proper.
This includes external fertilization and intra-uterine
implantation of ova. However, the Commission is not

41

prepared at this time to express an opinion in cases
where germ cells are derived from an unmarried couple or where gestation occurs in the uterus of another
woman.[3]

The commission's 1973 report repeats some of this language verbatim.

We believe that employment of artificial insemination
by husband and wife is morally licit and proper,
understanding that only the sperm derived from the
husband and the ova from the wife are used. This
includes external fertilization and intra-uterine
implantation of ova.

The 1982 report of the Commission on Human Affairs and
Health noted that some voices had been raised in objection to
IVF "on the basis that one is grossly interfering in the reproduction process, a process or physiological function which
some presume to have special protection."[5] The commission
believed this concern was unwarranted, however.

The normal parents, defeated in their efforts to
achieve pregnancy by normal routes are using physical means to assist in a normal life process. This does
not, on the face of it, appear to be subject to objections
on moral, theological, or ethical grounds any more
than the use of other prosthetic devices used to assist
in life processes such as artificial organs, limbs, or
implants.[6]

Again in 1988, the commission observed,

Anglican and Protestant ethics generally . . . affirm
A.I.H. as a means to help a married couple conceive
children. In this case the good of conception in marriage justifies these means to make conception possible.[7]

On the other hand, as these citations suggest, the use of
semen donated by a third party (AID) raises different issues.
The Joint Commission on the Church in Human Affairs in its
1973 report noted that:

There is serious question of the propriety of the use of
semen derived from a donor in situations where the
concept of the family is in question to begin with or
where it might be raised later.[8]

In contrast, the 1982 report expressly affirmed "the value
of surrogate parenting through the means of the anonymous
male donor" because "the wholeness of the marital union

brought about through wanted children must be valued above the risk."[9]

The softening toward AID continued in 1985. That year's report claimed that the church has not opposed artificial insemination, given that most couples' attitude toward procreation is loving and unselfish. But the report rejected the interjection of money into the process and the "congruence of consumerist values in personal relationships with technical advances in modern obstetrics"[10] that now enables purchase of embryos for implantation.

[T]o the extent that such an embryo is a person, a human being may soon be for sale. Can the Church condone the buying and selling of the flesh into which Christ came down from heaven?[11]

The flirtation with support for use of donor gametes ended in 1988. The commission noted, "Serious moral objections are raised by Christian ethicists about fertility enhancement by a third person."[12] The commission concluded that it "cannot affirm AID as a moral option for members of this Church."[13]

A new factor entered the commission's deliberations in the late 1980s with the expression of concerns about lineage—both social and biological. Thus, the 1988 report notes that an "anonymous" donor's "genetic expression and personhood will be part of any conception."[14] Hiding the donor parent denies the child knowledge of his or her biological ancestry and allows the donor to evade moral and legal responsibility. On the other hand, revealing the donor's identity to the child obviously raises "difficult issues of parenting, family identification for the child, and, potentially, legal issues of parental responsibility."[15]

A fourth element that has been mentioned in these reports is the importance of adoption as a desirable alternative. From the 1973 report:

Since the object of artificial insemination is the increase in the size of a family by circumventing blocks to normal conception and gestation, care should be given that the adoption of children now without the chance of normal family life be considered as one of the options available to such couples and families.[16]

Surrogate Motherhood

Another issue that has attracted significant attention from the church is surrogate motherhood. As early as 1973, the Joint Commission on the Church in Human Affairs asserted,

the use of a host uterus to obtain the gestation of a child outside the family almost necessarily involves the treatment of the second woman as a mere object.[17]

Concern with the exploitation of persons is a recurring theme. In 1982, the Commission on Human Affairs and Health distinguished between artificial insemination and surrogate motherhood. The differences are tacitly acknowledged by the prices charged for the two services (several hundred dollars versus tens of thousands of dollars, in the commission's formulation). The sperm donor's identity is unknown, and he forms no emotional attachment to the child who may be conceived, in contrast to the experience of the surrogate mother.

Certainly the natural mother must experience all the emotional, psychological, and physical changes associated with child-bearing that will force strong ties to the newborn, while, at the same time, she is being treated as a mindless child-bearing animal by the prospective recipient parents.[18]

Drawing an analogy between surrogacy and prostitution in its 1985 report, the commission observed: "Surrogate motherhood . . . needs to be examined in incarnational terms."[19] In the commission's view, surrogacy differs fundamentally from artificial insemination in terms of its emotional impact not only on the surrogate mother, but also upon her other children and the adoptive parents.

The commission appealed to various risks raised by surrogating arrangements. It granted the positive values of providing children to childless couples, in the absence of genetic problems or manipulative behavior of participants. But it also pointed to drawbacks. For example, the arrangement gives the natural parent a "very powerful lever" over the adoptive parent in situations of crisis or stress. The child conceived through surrogating also has a weapon against the adoptive parents.

In 1985, the commission pointed out that the Prayer Book's primary emphasis is on the relationship of husband and wife, their "mutual joy" and "the help and comfort given one another," with the procreation of children secondary, "when it is God's will." The commission observed, many infertile wives, considering a surrogate mother for their child, argue that their marriage cannot be fulfilled without a child. Clearly, that is not the view espoused in our liturgical formularies.[20]

The 1988 statement cast the issues in more theological terms, noting that

moral issues are usually discussed in American medicine and ethics outside any specifically Christian vision of marriage, parenting, and sexuality . . . due to the widespread secularization and indeed, secularism, of Western culture. . . . [The commission] cannot affirm surrogate motherhood as a moral option for members of this Church.[21]

Finally, and perhaps central to the whole tradition of its discussion of these matters, the commission appealed to the relational nature of sexuality as it is understood by the church. Thus, it rejected the use of technology to provide a child for a single person.

On the whole, this action appears to us to be in the mainstream of American narcissism and self-indulgence. The child is brought to a single person household for reasons of personal self-satisfaction and achievement rather than for the completion of God's holy union, and is to be condemned.[22]

The commission reiterated this position in its 1988 report, noting that a single woman conceiving her "own" child through AID and IVF is

"deliberately causing a child to suffer the deprivation and risks of having only one known biological parent." . . . These techniques place a primacy on having our baby or my baby over the care and nurturing of children. Is such a biologically biased view of parenting morally justified in the light of existing children needing adoption?[23]

In its most recent report to the 1991 General Convention, the Standing Commission on Health recommended that those who are considering the use of surrogates or donated gametes or embryos "should be urged to become thoroughly informed about the ethical issues involved and seek the counsel of a priest of this church."[24] The Convention passed a slightly amended version of the commission's draft resolution to that effect (Resolution A–101a).

However, the commission declined to take a stand on the

question, neither endorsing nor condemning these practices:
The Standing Commissions on Human Affairs and
Health of the Episcopal Church have expressed grave
doubts about these methods of having children, but
General Convention has neither approved nor condemned these practices that have potential both for
good and evil. Being wary of absolutes and open to
change has been an unstated policy of this Church. We
value this openness. If we attempt to overcontrol—to
prohibit the unfamiliar—we stifle creativity and make
it impossible for anyone to give us anything new. It
seems inappropriate at this time either to affirm or
denounce surrogacy or use of donated sperm, ova or
embryos.[25]

Problems in Teachings

What are we to make of this history? On balance, our judgment is that it could be worse, but that it could and should be
much better. The work raises two problems: inconsistency and
omission. The inconsistencies appear in the commission's
waffling on AID, which received some level of support for an
interval of about five years, after a period of opposition and
before a time of renewed rejection. Still, AID raises difficult
issues on which thoughtful persons might be expected to disagree. That a church with changing membership would shift
its ground over a twenty-year period is scarcely surprising.

The issue of omission is more troubling. First, none of
these commission reports seriously addresses the theological
question of the nature of embodied personhood. This issue
underlies the debate over abortion and the definition of death.
In particular, it is raised by the existence of embryos preserved by freezing for later implantation. Are these human
beings? Human persons? One very important school of
thought in recent bioethics argues that in order to be a person
one must have the capacity to take responsibility for one's
own actions. Is that a perspective that the commission, speaking for the church, can accept? Or are we committed to a more
inclusive understanding of who counts as a person? Oliver
O'Donovan, Regius Professor of Moral Theology at Oxford,
argues that a broader view fits much better with the rich concept of person used in our historic doctrine of God.[26]

Second, these procedures raise questions about the role of
reproduction in marriage that the commission has only begun

to address. On the one hand, these questions concern the necessity of children for the fulfillment or completion of a marriage. Childless marriage, including chosen childless marriage, is a valid marriage even in conservative Roman Catholic moral theology. What is the commission's stance on this point? At stake is the relative importance of reproduction versus companionship or mutual love as the essence of marriage. We have one theology of marriage if reproduction is required, another if the capacity to reproduce together is essential, and still another if reproductive capacity is irrelevant.

On the other hand, this line of inquiry forces the church to come to terms with the question of the extent to which it has canonized the nuclear family as the Christian lifestyle par excellence. To what extent does the church's teaching and communal life support single or childless persons in their vocations? Why are young people surprised to discover that the church does not think the gift of children—especially of one's own biological children—is something one must have, whatever the price?

The relationship between a married couple is not the only issue. At least since F.D. Maurice, one important strand of Anglican moral theology has stressed the relational nature of human selfhood. But what does a relationship involve? Is it strictly a meeting of the minds? Is pregnancy to be understood as a human relationship in this constitutive sense? One can scarcely speak of mutual understanding between fetus and pregnant woman, but there is interaction, mutual influence, dependence. Or should pregnancy be understood as a matter of ownership? It is hard to say much about surrogacy without thorough investigation of these questions.

Another issue concerns the identity of the child. Surrogacy and AID are not the only practices that entail a separation of biological and social roots. Adoption does as well. In *Begotten or Made?*, O'Donovan argues that it is important to retain a sense that it is the adopting (perhaps childless) couple who are doing a favor. The whole moral color of the procedure is changed if the ultimate rationale is assistance to the adopting couple. Giving up a child for adoption can be an act of moral courage. It is one thing when a parent acts out of love, motivated to surrender the child by considerations of its best interests—the case in traditional adoptions. It's quite another thing deliberately to engender a child for the sake of other parties—the case in surrogating. The latter course reduces the child to the means to an end. Can we provide a rationale for adoption that does not sanction surrogacy?

Finally, the commission has been unable to give much time to discussion of the psychological and economic costs of the quest for fertility. The IVF procedures have a limited success rate, and therapeutic techniques may be embarrassing and uncomfortable. The technologies have a high price tag: as things stand, the more advanced procedures (beyond AI) are available only to persons with access to tens of thousands of dollars. This fact must raise questions about the constitution of our community and about what constitutes a basic medical need that the community must meet. Is there a right to fertility? What sacrifices may one of us be asked to make (e.g., in tax money) to ensure a child to another? What is justice in reproduction?

These issues are new and difficult; they are certainly not easily resolvable, and Christian tradition has not addressed many of them. But the broader issues of sex and marriage were explored by all the great theologians from Augustine through Barth. This diverse tradition, however, does not seem to have been a major conversation partner of the Episcopal commission. Indeed, there is no apparent reference to parallel work by our Lutheran and Catholic ecumenical conversation partners. But dialogue with them might have forced us into examining the theological dimensions of problems in reproductive ethics. Similarly, secular bioethics has been excluded from the church's deliberations of these questions, although the vigorous discussions of the past generation in that context might be expected to contribute some insights.

In short, the church has considered issues raised by the technologies of assisted reproduction apart from both the theological ethical traditions that are its birthright and the mainstream public discussion of biomedical ethics. It has chosen repeatedly to comment on intimate and anguishing matters touching closely on the identities of persons without adequately laying the foundation for its concern. In order to justify speaking about problems like the new technologies for reproduction the church must have something to say about them. There must be conceptual, theological, philosophical, and moral resources on which it can draw.

We take the view that the church speaks because it is identified with the cause of the God who liberates, calls to discipleship, and exercises sovereignty. The theological symbols of creation, exodus and covenant structure a self-understanding that requires concern for the welfare of human persons. For centuries these symbols have informed the way Christians think together about God's sovereignty and procreation, the liberation and salvation of persons, and the covenants that bind us together. Indifference to human suffering is un-Christian.

On the other hand, although these symbols provide parameters, they are not sufficient in themselves to settle questions of what the church should stand for. They must be translated[27] into value terms like liberty, loyalty, and the natural as an ideal. The church should stand for a community of humankind that has certain characteristics: liberty is revered, commitments are honored, human (and nonhuman) nature is respected. Thus, we think it important for the church's discussion of new technologies for reproduction (as of all issues) to be rational and reasonable, intelligible to non-Christians who may want to argue with church speech.

Translation is necessary not only because the church operates in a foreign and hostile external world. Moral speech is not just a part of the church's foreign policy; it is part of the internal life of the community. Translation is also necessary so that we can talk honestly to each other. Speech using the rich and full language of our constitution and tradition is appropriate in public, secular contexts, for example, when we appeal to a national covenant or celebrate a sense of America as a Garden of Eden that may be despoiled.

We realize that our assertions about theological method in ethics will require a more extended defense on another occasion. We include them here simply to show why the commission's failure to relate its work either to the secular or the theological context is so striking. The inconsistencies and omissions in its discussions largely flow from the absence of serious intellectual conversation partners from the Christian past, the ecumenical world, or the contemporary moral and medical community. Talking to a parent, sibling, or neighbor is richer than talking to oneself.

Problems of Structure and Procedure

These substantive issues reflect a serious structural and procedural problem. The commission that has addressed AID and IVF had many other assignments on its plate. The issues of abortion and the ordination and marriage of homosexual persons dominated its agenda during the period. It met infrequently; it had a limited budget; and its membership, which comprised thoughtful church leaders, included very few persons who had special expertise in the study of any of the issues before it.

Yet during this same period the body of literature called bioethics was a growth industry.[28] Major national and international scholarly bodies were wrestling with these issues,[29] and other branches of the Anglican communion were producing documents of significant technical sophistication and intellectual depth.[30]

We must ask whether the current structure provides the best way for the church to respond to issues raised by the new technologies for reproduction. Although we are in an era of rapid technological change, the basic facts about surrogating and artificial insemination have not changed significantly. Is the best response to these practices a brief new statement issued at three-year intervals? Would we not have been much better served by a more rigorous and weighty statement that was allowed to occupy some social space for a significant interval?

These are strong words, especially when they are occasioned by a series of reports that *for what they are* are of high quality—and with which, incidentally, we largely agree. The problem is structural and fundamental. When major nonreligious groups invest years of work and considerable resources in wrestling with hard moral questions, it is inconceivable that church commissions can do better on a shoestring. It's asking too much of the Holy Spirit! A public statement—and the commission's reports are public statements—that has not visibly been informed by a sustained and even-handed process of inquiry and that fails to capitalize on medical, scientific, moral, and theological expertise can only discredit the cause it seeks to advance. This is not to say that the church needs to redo the entire public process, only that it must make use of available expertise and that it must be visibly willing to proceed in a genuinely humble spirit of inquiry.

If the church's process on these matters has gone wrong, the reason may lie in a mistaken view of the origin or development of the church's moral teaching. In Catholic tradition it is common to distinguish the *ordinary* magisterium, or teaching authority, of the church from the *extraordinary* magisterium. Most matters of faith and morals rest on the ordinary magisterium, a kind of consensus of the faithful. Extraordinary action, or formal doctrinal definition, is undertaken when an acute controversy has arisen and where it is essential to the life of the church that the controversy be resolved. Given this distinction, we take the view that on questions of biomedical ethics the ordinary magisterium should control in the Episcopal Church. That is, the community requires instruction and time in order to see clearly what the issues are. It may turn out that this process of percolation of the issues—of educated discussion in the church—eventually requires formal resolution by General Convention or the House of Bishops, but that act of the extraordinary magisterium should be a last resort, rather than the starting point in the social process.

Our point is not that the issues raised by reproductive technologies should be ignored, but that our tradition supports a better, if slower, way of responding to them than these commission reports manifest. Earlier in this century, Kenneth Kirk argued that the genius of the Church of England was the stress it placed on custom. Kirk was clear that accidents of history were responsible for this fortunate development.[31] We think the Episcopal Church in the United States would intentionally adopt this more cautious style. Instead of thinking in terms of the quasi-legislative mode and formulating resolutions, we should stress a kind of common law mentality in which we eschew grand statements of principle, trusting rather that moral truth will emerge in educated grapplings with problems by Christians. Consensus is not to be manufactured; it happens, and the process will not be rushed or engineered.

Failure to embrace this more patient approach puts our official statements in a strange position. Has the Episcopal Church said that participants in AID are doing something unChristian? Should such a person withdraw from communion? Or is this a topic where church teaching is in doubt? We are uncomfortable taking a hard line on these issues for good reasons, and we should not, in our public pronouncements, claim for the church a degree of certainty it does not have. We should not escalate the issues into inappropriately—or prematurely—high stakes.

The worst problem with the misdirection of energy and attention toward resolutions is that we avoid the more fundamental educational task. Concentration on statements at the national or judicatory level can divert attention from the more fundamental task of nourishing discussion and exploration within congregations of inquiring Christian persons. During the time these commission statements were produced, we wonder how many adult education classes discussed the issues in any depth.[32] In a word, a commission statement is what Bonhoeffer called "cheap grace." It's easy, and it gives the sense that something has been done when in reality the actual engagement of the church is avoided.

In brief, we think the Episcopal Church should be spending more time talking about issues such as AID and IVF and less time trying to settle these questions in plenary sessions at General Convention.[33] We should acknowledge frankly that the church as a whole is in a process of inquiry, and we should not be afraid to consult relevant expertise on these issues. We need knowledgeable spokespersons speaking in a leadership capacity, trying to guide the church. And we should acknowledge the legitimacy of various forms of disagreement.

We think church resources should be redirected so as to support a series of working parties that would address issues of obvious importance (for example, care of the dying, access to health care, abortion, and the new technologies for reproduction). These statements should simply carry the authority that the names of their authors bring to them. Each working party should include experts in medicine, law, ethics, and theology; each should have a limited time frame to produce a short position paper readable to all; each should be provided with adequate budget resources for travel and staff support. Appropriate models are the Warnock Commission in the United Kingdom or the study group that drafted *On Dying Well*. Of course, not all will agree with the reports produced by these commissions. But they will be significant statements in their own right, and they will serve as a significant catalyst for discussion throughout the church. Leaders of the church will be speaking, but they will not be the bishops or convention delegates, and they will not be speaking in a way that appears to commit the whole denomination.

Endnotes

1. The technologies of assisted reproduction produce significant permutations and combinations in parenting. Sperm and ovum can now be united in vitro and implanted in a uterus

that may or may not belong to the donor of the ovum. Embryos can be preserved by freezing; they can be tested for defects before implantation; they have been the subject of custody suits. The new technologies inevitably raise profound questions about parenting, the moral status of the early embryo, the weight to be assigned to the desire to have a child, the exploitation of donors (or persons or gametes), and the existence of property rights in one's progeny.

2. The discussion that follows is based primarily on the reports of various bodies (including the Joint Commission on the Church in Human Affairs, the Joint Commission on Religion and Health, and the Standing Committee on Human Affairs and Health) between 1973 and 1988.

3. The discussion of assisted reproduction comprises one paragraph in a report of approximately twenty pages. The bulk of the report is devoted to issues confronting humankind in a technological age (including concerns about computers taking over decision making), and questions of justice (including equitable access to medical care). *Journal of the General Convention*, 1970, p. 467.

4. *Journal of the General Convention*, 1973, p. 595.

5. *The Blue Book,* 1982, p. 134.

6. Ibid.

7. *The Blue Book*, 1988, p. 158.

8. *Journal of the General Convention*, 1973, p. 595.

9. *The Blue Book*, 1982, p. 133.

10. *The Blue Book*, 1985, p. 141.

11. Ibid.

12. *The Blue Book*, 1988, p. 158.

13. Ibid., p. 159.

14. Ibid., p. 158.

15. Ibid.

16. *Journal of the General Convention*, 1973, p. 595.

17. Ibid.

18. *The Blue Book*, 1982, p. 133.

19. *The Blue Book*, 1985, p. 141.

20. Ibid., p. 142.

21. *The Blue Book*, 1988, p. 159.

22. *The Blue Book*, 1982, p. 133.

23. *The Blue Book*, 1988, p. 159.

24. Sjoerd L. Bonting, ed., "Health Concerns: Report and Background Material Prepared by the Standing Commission on Health of the Episcopal Church," San Francisco, 27 June 1991, p. 13.

25. Ibid.

26. Oliver O'Donovan, *Begotten or Made?* (New York: Oxford University Press, 1984), pp. 49–66.

27. John C. Bennett's work on the importance of this translation process remains an important contribution by a leader of the ecumenical and neo-orthodox movements. See the references collected in David H. Smith, *The Achievement of John C. Bennett* (New York: Herder and Herder, 1970).

28. See the *Encyclopedia of Bioethics*, the annual *Bibliography of Bioethics*, and *The Hastings Center Report.*

29. For example, see President's Commission for the Study of Ethical Problems in Medicine and Biomedical and Behavioral Research, *Screening and Counseling for Genetic Conditions* (Washington, D.C.: Government Printing Office, 1983) and Ethics Advisory Board, Department of Health, Education, and Welfare, *Report and Conclusions: HEW Support of Research Involving Human In Vitro Fertilization and Embryo Transfer* (Washington, D.C.: Government Printing Office, 1979).

30. For example: Mary Warnock, *Report of the Committee of Inquiry into Human Fertilization and Embryology* (London: Her Majesty's Stationery Office, July 1984); Working Party, *On Dying Well: An Anglican Contribution to the Debate on Euthanasia*, (London: Church Information Office, 1975); the *Journal of Medical Ethics*, which was nurtured in the Church of England; Church in Wales Board of Mission, Division for Social Responsibility, *Human Infertility Services and Embryology: Some Ethical Issues* (Penarth: Church in Wales Publications, 1989); and R.A. Gillies, "Report of a Working Party on Human Infertility and Embryo Research," Scottish Episcopal Church (mimeograph), 31 May 1987.

31. Kenneth Kirk, *Ignorance, Faith and Conformity: Studies in Moral Theology* (London: Longmans, Green & Co., 1925).

32. One example of pertinent material produced for use in congregations of the Episcopal Church is David A. Ames and Colin B. Gracey, eds., *Good Genes* (Cincinnati: Forward Movement Publications, 1984).

33. It may be worth noting that the 1988 General Convention considered a resolution urging study of the issue at the diocesan level. The text is as follows:

> *Resolved*, . . . That this 69th General Convention commend medical researchers and practitioners, ethicists and theologians, lawyers, counselors, clergy and all men and women who study with care the spiritual and moral dilemmas of assisted parenting, which includes surrogate parenting; and be it further
>
> *Resolved*, That this General Convention advise all members of our Church who are considering such parenthood to consult informed clergy or other counselors in its spiritual as well as psychological dimensions; and be it further
>
> *Resolved*, That this General Convention encourage full study and discussion in each diocese of the spiritual and moral issues of assisted parenting, including the welfare of children so conceived; and be it further
>
> *Resolved*, That this General Convention request each diocesan bishop to undertake the identification and training of informed clergy and counselors and report the work done to the Standing Commission on Human Affairs and Health no later than September 30, 1990. *Journal of the General Convention*, 1988, pp. 634–635.

3

Changing Teachings on Abortion

David A. Scott

Since 1967 the Episcopal Church has consistently addressed abortion in its public teaching, largely through resolutions from General Convention. These resolutions are confused in their goals, their intended audience, and their language. Marred by tensions in logic, the resolutions avoid fundamental issues related to abortion and fail to identify standards which should guide moral conscience. The inadequacy of these resolutions lies not only in their content but also in the constraints on moral education imposed by the resolution as a form of communication. The limitations connected with resolutions raise the question of whether this form of communication should be the means by which the church seeks to educate the conscience of its members.

As alternatives to resolutions, a range of different forms of teaching exists in the Episcopal Church. For example, individuals who either teach in Episcopal seminaries and/or are members of the Episcopal Church provide moral teaching through articles and books. Two examples of such writings on abortion are given by Timothy Sedgwick and David Smith.[1] Moral teaching is also done in ethics courses in Episcopal seminaries. Diocesan committees convened to study abortion and foster discussion and teaching on the topic in congregations have also provided a variety of resources, including videos, study guides, and essays.[2]

The variety of levels and forms at and through which moral teaching occurs in the church is reflected in the history of Anglicanism. In its formative years, Anglicanism understood moral education as a necessary task of the church. The goal was to form the conscience, individually and socially, of the whole church. As reformed, the Church of England did not confine its formal moral instruction to priests in the context of hearing confessions. Rather, through sermons, lectures, books, cases of conscience, and learned treatises written in the vernacular, the church sought to instruct the whole people of God, the laity as well as the ordained. Already in the sixteenth century, for example, moral teaching is given in the Books of Homilies; in the seventeenth century moral teaching is most notably given through the works of individual Anglican Divines such as Joseph Hall, Jeremy Taylor, and Robert Sanderson.

While teachings, from sermons to adult forums, must address and engage the people of God at the level of the congregation, they serve discussion and debate on moral issues and form conscience only when they are informed by moral teachings reflecting those of the larger church. It is this body of teaching that is now lacking, and for this reason it is a mistake to assume that resolutions passed by General Convention reflect the mind of the church. What these resolutions do is to reveal the questions and issues the church must address, whether through teachings in the church or through teachings by the church.

In view of a study of the resolutions on abortion I will argue that resolutions are not the best medium for the church to form Christian conscience. Formulated by a few people and passed at a national meeting, resolutions abstract from the process of moral formulation which must go on throughout the whole church. Second, while I will urge that bishops should play a greater role than they now do in the Episcopal Church's teaching, their role must be understood to include rather than preempt the process of moral debate and dialogue which ought to proceed at all levels of the church through a variety of forms.

Resolutions from General Convention
Current teaching on abortion begins with the 1967 resolution passed before the historic 1973 *Roe v. Wade* Supreme Court decision legalizing unrestricted access to clinical abortions during the first trimester of pregnancy. The resolution affirmed the need for

> abortion-law reform, to permit the termination of pregnancy, where the decision to terminate has been arrived at with proper safeguards against abuse, and where it has been clearly established that the physical health of the mother is threatened seriously, or where

there is substantial reason to believe that the child would be born badly deformed in mind or body, or where the pregnancy has resulted from forcible rape or incest.[3]

In light of the 1973 Supreme Court decision, the General Convention meeting in Minneapolis in 1976 shifted the focus of its teaching from the reform of civil laws restricting abortion to the support of civil law legalizing abortion and the support of the individual person confronting the choice of elective abortion. After underscoring the moral seriousness of all actions which can lead to the beginning of new life, the resolution affirms deliberate limiting of family size and the practice of responsible birth control as aspects of Christian moral responsibility regarding the beginning of new life. "Abortions for convenience" are explicitly excluded as a "moral limitation" on family size.

The 1976 resolution goes on to affirm the 1967 resolution; however, it cites the form of the resolution which was not passed by that Convention when it affirms "support for 'termination of pregnancy' particularly in those cases where 'the physical or mental health of the mother is threatened seriously, or where there is substantial reason to believe that the child would be born badly deformed in mind or body, or where the pregnancy has resulted from rape or incest.' "[4] (This inaccurate citation of the 1967 resolution passed in 1976 and was repeated in resolutions passed by the General Conventions in 1979 and 1982.)[5]

Finally, the resolution from 1976 urged Episcopalians seeking abortions for reasons other than those stated "to seek the advice and counsel of a Priest, . . . and, where appropriate, penance." Episcopalians are to explore "other preferable courses of action." And, again, "The Episcopal Church express[es] its unequivocal opposition to any legislation on the part of the national or state governments which would abridge or deny the right of individuals to reach informed decisions in this matter and to act upon them."[6]

In the subsequent General Conventions in 1979 and 1982, the 1976 resolution was reaffirmed. In 1985 the General Convention again "commended the Church's official position adopted at Convention in 1976, 1979 and 1982," and "requested the dioceses to initiate studies of the pastoral, personal, sociological and theological implications of abortion."[7]

Thus, until the 1988 General Convention, the 1976 resolution was the most official Episcopal Church teaching on abortion. As requested, in its report for the Blue Book for deputies to the 1988 General Convention, the (then named) Standing Commission on Human Affairs and Health reported feedback from dioceses about the Episcopal Church's teaching on abortion. The report stated that most Episcopalians interviewed supported the major thrust of the resolution on abortion. Those who did not support the resolution argued that when permission for abortion was given it seemed to recommend abortion. Also, some thought that the resolution implied that all potentially disabled babies should be aborted. The report stated that many Episcopalians were frustrated by the "vagueness and lack of clarity of the resolution."[8]

To my knowledge, no evidence exists that the Standing Commission on Human Affairs or the bishops or any other group in the church asked what was the purpose for gathering information from dioceses about opinions concerning Episcopal teaching on abortion. Did the General Convention's request that such feedback be gathered imply some conception of theology by plebiscite? That is, was the premise that if wide disagreement to the current abortion teaching was discovered, the teaching should be changed? Or was the assumption that if Episcopalians seemed generally satisfied with the then current resolution, then the teaching was true and should not be changed? This is an important question. The notion of theology by plebiscite is, in fact, one conceivable answer to the basic questions being raised in this book—questions such as what is the purpose of the church's moral teaching, to whom is it addressed, and who should state that teaching?

As the response from dioceses indicated, convictions from the church-at-large were far more diverse than suggested by the resolutions passed by General Convention from 1967 through 1985. Some of these differences were reflected in the new claims that the Commission on Human Affairs and Health proposed in the resolution it presented to the 1988 General Convention. The proposed resolution affirmed that all human life is sacred from its inception until death; it urged the church to take seriously its obligation to help form the consciences of its members; and it acknowledged couples who have borne, loved, and cared for seriously disabled children. The resolution also reaffirmed as moral the decision for termination of pregnancy in specific instances—the threat to the health of the mother, serious disability of the child, and in cases of rape and incest. In this light, legislators were urged to respect individual consciences. Always, the resolution said, abortion has a tragic dimension. Finally, the resolution deplored abortions after viability, as well as the large number of abortions.

A second resolution was also submitted by the Standing Commission on Human Affairs. This resolution emphatically opposed "abortion as a means of birth control, family planning, sex selection, or any reason of mere convenience."[9] However, these changes from earlier resolutions were insufficient for many at the Convention. In committee meetings and on the floor of Convention, the Standing Commission's 1988 draft resolution was considered too permissive regarding morally acceptable reasons for abortion, affirming as it did the earlier resolutions dating back to 1967. Deputies of the Diocese of Virginia proposed an alternative resolution. In the end, in fact, the final resolution passed by General Convention included the first and last paragraphs from the commission's draft and included paragraphs two through eight of the alternative resolution. The result was a strikingly different resolution from any the Episcopal Church has previously passed.

Unlike the previous resolutions on abortion, the 1988 resolution claimed that congregations have responsibility to "assist their members in becoming informed concerning the spiritual, physiological and psychological aspects of sex and sexuality." The church, moreover, was seen as having an "obligation to help form the consciences of its members concerning this sacredness [of human life]." Church members, especially clergy, were called upon "to become aware of local agencies and resources which will assist those faced with problem pregnancies." The resolution also referred to the *Book of Common Prayer's* affirmation that the birth of a child is a joyous and solemn occasion for families and for the Christian community. Finally, removed from this 1988 resolution was any reference to earlier resolutions on abortion. Any indication of the situations in which abortion would be morally permissible were eliminated. Absent also were the previous admonitions "to seek the advice and counsel of a Priest of this Church, and, where appropriate, penance."

Ecclesial Shifts in Perspective

The specific changes in the 1988 resolution from previous resolutions on abortion reflect three fundamental shifts in perspective. First, the 1988 resolution is clear about the audience the church addresses. The resolutions from 1967 through 1982 are addressed to no one in particular. Their opening paragraphs identify neither who speaks nor who is addressed. By contrast, the 1988 resolution is more explicit. The second sentence states, "The Church takes seriously its obligation to help form the consciences of its members concerning this sacredness" of all human life "from its inception until death." The "speaker" of the resolution is the Christian church; "addressed" are members of the Christian church. In this light, the purpose of such teaching is clearly stated: to help "form the consciences of its members." With this statement the resolution claims that the Christian community has an obligation to help shape the moral conscience of its members and, by implication, that the church has the competency and the right to do so.

This focus on the church is further reflected in the claim that congregations are responsible to assist their members in learning "the spiritual, physiological and psychological aspects of sex and sexuality." Noteworthy in this shift is the emphasis placed upon the local congregation. In turn, the local congregation is assigned competency and authority.

A second shift from earlier resolutions on abortion to the 1988 resolution is the change in emphasis from drawing boundaries between the morally permissible and impermissible to stressing the positive good of childbirth and the evil of abortion. The introduction to the resolution itself describes the resolution as a statement not on abortion but on "childbirth and abortion." Quoting from the *Book of Common Prayer*, the resolution affirms that "the birth of a child is a joyous and solemn occasion in the life of a family" and for the whole Christian community. Abortion is then placed in contrast to this positive good, "as having a tragic dimension, calling for the concern and compassion of all the Christian community."

The 1988 resolution presents criteria for abortions that would be morally wrong: "as a means of birth control, family planning, sex selection, or any reason of mere convenience." Instead of limiting the resolution to the morally permissible, the resolution then goes on to specify "positive courses of action, including, but not limited to . . . the parents raising the child; another family member raising the child; [and] making the child available for adoption." Finally, the resolution instructs Christians, especially clergy, to be informed of local agencies and resources for those with problem pregnancies. Thus, whereas the earlier resolutions focused on drawing the boundary separating morally permissible and morally imper- missible abortions, the 1988 resolution directs the Christian reader toward alternatives to abortions.

A third shift in the teaching of this resolution is from advocating civil legislation legalizing abortion to urging legis- lators to respect individual moral conscience. Resolutions from 1976 through 1982 declared unequivocal opposition to any legislation abridging the right of individuals to act upon decisions concerning abortion. In fact, these resolutions advo- cated the legal status quo after the 1973 *Roe v. Wade* decision, and implied that anyone who wanted to reverse the *Roe v. Wade* decision regarding access to abortion had an illicit moral intention. In contrast, the 1988 resolution takes no stand regarding the existing civil legislation on abortion. Instead, by stating that "legislation concerning abortions will not address the root of the problem," the 1988 resolution dis- tinguishes between what is legal and what is moral and then side-steps taking a position for or against current legislation.

These three shifts in focus in the 1988 resolution from pre- vious resolutions on abortion create a more ecclesial empha- sis. The 1988 resolution on abortion is an ecclesial document, a statement in the church, by the church, for the church, based on the church's theological and moral standards. The resolu- tion's stated purpose is to help the church form the con- science of its members; it affirms a specific good, the birth of children in families and within the Christian community; and its only appeal to a standard is to a document of Christian tra- dition in the Episcopal Church, the *Book of Common Prayer.*

Problems with the 1988 Resolution

While clearer in its intent as an ecclesial document, how- ever, the 1988 resolution gives only superficial moral guid- ance to those who turn to it for help, and what guidance it does give is inadequate. The resolution, moreover, fails to draw logical conclusions from what it says, evades substantive issues, and fails to make an adequate appeal to the grounds for its teachings.

One logical tension, if not inconsistency, in the 1988 resolution is between "emphatically [opposing] abortions as a means of birth control, family planning, sex selection, or any reason of mere convenience" and failing to oppose the *Roe v. Wade* ruling which allows elective abortion for any reason. If it is morally wrong for a person to elect an abortion, say for sex selection, *Roe v. Wade* (which allows an abortion for any reason in the first trimester) appears at least prima facie immoral.

It might be claimed that the resolution's belief that "legislation concerning abortions will not address the root of the problem" saves the resolution from inconsistency if not outright contradiction. A defender of the resolution's coherence might claim that it does not imply that all legal abortions are moral. It only says that abortion legislation does not go to the heart of the problem and, therefore, does not take any position about the morality of all legal abortions. Nevertheless, the logical coherence of the resolution remains muddy. At the least, the absence of any stand on the legislative question conflicts with the affirmative position toward the same legislation in previous abortion resolutions. At the most, a logical tension, if not an outright contradiction, exists in the 1988 resolution's opposition to abortion for certain reasons which are allowed by current legislation.

A second problem of logical coherence resides in the resolution's affirmation of the sacredness of all human life. If all human life is sacred and if fetal life is human life, how can a woman elect to destroy the life of the fetus, even "in extreme situations?" A defender of the resolution's coherence might respond that the phrase "from its inception" saves the resolution from contradiction. The fetus is not human life, this defense could maintain, and, therefore, "sacredness" is not an attribute of the fetus. Yet, if the fetus is not human life, the resolution need not have begun with the statement that all human life is sacred from its inception until death. To do so, if the fetus is not human, is to announce a principle irrelevant to abortion and the resolution. While we may then assume that the resolution claims that fetal life is human, the problem remains: if fetal life is sacred, is it not prima facie wrong to destroy it, even in extreme situations?

A defender of the coherence of the resolution might still respond that sacred implies worthy of respect and reverence, but not inviolable. That is, the life of the fetus, because sacred, may only be destroyed in extreme situations, not for "any rea-son of mere convenience." The defender might go on to point out that while Christianity affirms the sacredness of all human life, it does allow killing in self-defense and in the context of justifiable war. Again, the point of this defense turns on the meaning of "sacred," that the attribute of sacredness applied to human life does not entail the moral consequence of absolute inviolability. Appeal to the tradition of justifiable war and licitness of self-defense is vulnerable, however, to the obvious point that killing in war and in self-defense is arguably licit only because the human being killed is an unjust aggressor, not an innocent victim. For the appeal to jus-tifiable war or self-defense to work, the defender of the resolu-tion must successfully defend the claim that a fetus is an unjust aggressor. Yet, obviously, a fetus cannot have the immoral intent to attack an innocent person.

Probably the strongest defense to be made for the logical coherence of the resolution is to claim that sacred means wor-thy of respect and protection, but that even innocent human life is not an absolute good and in some situations even inno-cent life may be sacrificed for proportional reasons—for exam-ple, to save the life of the mother. Hence, it is logically coherent to argue both that human life, including fetal life, is sacred *and* that in some situations we may deliberately destroy human life. This defense has the merit of making the language of sacredness coherent with the resolution's claim that "all abortion [has] a tragic dimension." Redeeming the coherence of the resolution, if possible on this point, requires a fuller theological and moral argument than is given. General Convention resolutions may simply not be the right form for the development of such reasoning and, more broadly, for moral education.

A final contradiction in the 1988 resolution is present in the statement that "we oppose abortion as a means of birth control." In fact, the intention of the moral agent who has an induced abortion is always birth control. An induced abortion in fact interrupts the normal biological process of gestation leading to birth. People choose induced abortions to control birth. One might respond that the resolution actually means to condemn the choice of abortion as a substitute or alternative to artificial means of birth control. This is cogent only on the assumption that birth control is licit and raises the question of why. The answer can only be that artificial means of birth control do not involve the destruction of an existing human life, which is immoral. This returns the discussion to the logical tension named above: if taking human life is immoral, why does the resolution not condemn all elective abortions, since every elective abortion is the intentional destruction of a human life.

In addition to the problem of coherence, the 1988 resolution evades fundamental issues related to abortion. By evasion I mean the intentional failure to address an issue which obviously pertains to the subject of abortion and clearly affects persons to whom the resolution is addressed. The most notable evasion in the resolution is in the opening statement that human life is sacred "from its inception until death." This fails to answer the question, When does fetal life acquire the attributes of sacredness? This issue is central in informing moral decisions about abortion and directly affects Episcopalians who are contemplating abortion or who, as health care professionals, are involved or might be involved in performing abortions. These persons may look to the church for moral guidance; instead, they find that the church fails to give clear guidance about when sacredness should be attributed to human life.

On the one hand, as we said above, if fetal life is not human life and therefore sacred, it would be superfluous for the resolution about childbirth and abortion to begin by stating the principle that all human life is sacred from its inception until its death. The clear implication of that statement is that fetal life is human life, and therefore the abortion decision concerns human life which is sacred. Yet, the resolution obfuscates that implication when it uses the word inception rather than conception. Had conception rather than inception been used, a clear temporal point would be identified from which time sacredness should be attributed to human life. With a definite temporal beginning designated, the term conception would complement "death," which also designates a clearly temporal point in time, at least when referring to whole brain death. Inception, however, has no clear temporal reference.

What, then, we are left to ponder, does inception mean? Does it mean conception? Biologically, conception means the fusion of egg and sperm and/or implantation of the fertilized egg (the zygote) in the uterine wall. In any case, conception is the biological beginning of new human life. At the purely linguistic level, a case could be made that inception must mean conception. The dictionary definition of inception is "to commence" or "to begin." Human life begins at conception; therefore, inception must refer to the biological event of conception. Yet the resolution chooses the word inception.

The resolution could have said instead that it doesn't know whether fetal life is human life and sacred. This would have the merit of honesty, a merit reinforced by the fact that the moral status of the fetus is a topic of moral dispute. The failure to acknowledge this problem and to use inception can only be interpreted as an evasion, one might say evasion by equivocation.

The use of the word inception is not the only case of avoidance or evasion of moral issues that are central to addressing abortion. The resolution also evades or avoids feminist concerns. The resolution says nothing about the link between a woman's legal access to abortion and the issue of justice and equality for women in society. Yet this is a fundamental theme of Beverly Harrison's book on abortion, *Our Right to Choose*.[10] The resolution affirms the birth of children but says nothing related to the sexual lives of women. Completely absent from the resolution is any reference to the sexual denigration and abuse of women, to the problems of rape, incest, and psychological exploitation of women by men. Because of such violence and denigration, support for legalized abortion is for some women a litmus test of respect for women.[11] Clearly, again, no one resolution can deal with all these important moral concerns. Once more there remains the question of what medium is appropriate for moral teaching in the Episcopal Church.

Finally, apart from one reference to the *Book of Common Prayer*, the 1988 resolution never cites a standard or basis for its moral claims. The traditional Anglican appeal to scripture, tradition, and reason finds little voice in the resolution. On what grounds must the church say that "human life is sacred from its inception until death?" On what basis must Christians "affirm responsible family planning?" Why should individual conscience be respected? No grounds are even named, much less developed, in making these claims.[12] The obvious point is that no resolution can give sufficient attention to these basic moral questions. Equally obvious, resolutions cannot be the sole, much less primary, source of moral teaching in the church.

What Needs to Be Done

Fundamentally, the Episcopal Church needs to raise and answer the question about its teaching authority. Does the Episcopal Church have a magisterial authority, a right, competence, and obligation to teach its members? This question of the church's teaching authority implies nothing less than the question of what the church is. Is the church an aggregate of individuals with similar religious opinions, a free association joined by common interests? If so, the justification for institutional discipline and intentional instruction of conscience is very different from the church as the body of Christ, whose members have the mind of Christ and are to mature into the fullness of that mind.

Anglicanism has understood the church not as a free association of religiously like-minded individuals, but as the body of Christ. And it has assigned to the order of bishops the responsibility "to guard the faith, unity and discipline of the Church." The question of teaching authority, therefore, concerns the role of bishops as teachers and as administrators of the discipline of the church. The Episcopal Church urgently needs to explore this role. In this exploration, at least the following questions and considerations are relevant.

First, what are the necessary conditions for bishops to fulfill their roles as pastors, teachers, and guardians of the faith? Clearly there must be a "critical mass" of bishops who have the intellectual gifts, academic training, and technical competence to understand and articulate theological and moral issues. Also, bishops must be able to assume willingly this role in good conscience.

A second set of questions concerns the nature of teaching and authority in the Anglican communion. Conceivably the bishops' teaching authority could be understood to reside in the office of bishop as such. According to this view, "the faithful" should accept the teaching of bishops on moral issues because the bishops teach a particular moral position. A position like this one, however, goes very much against the Anglican grain. Such a stance comes very close to an authoritarianism which Anglicanism has rejected. The traditional Anglican appeal to reason at least implies that the authority of teaching resides not just in the virtue of its author but also in the arguments themselves. This means that the bishops' teaching office requires them to confront basic issues of how the traditional sources of theology and ethics—scripture, tradition, and reason—are to be understood and applied to contemporary issues. Unless this is done, what bishops teach has no hope of persuading on its own merits.

The inadequacies of the 1988 resolution on abortion make clear that some other medium than General Convention resolutions needs to be found if the church is to teach. Resolutions are subject to the dynamics of political compromise and hasty choices inevitable in the context of General Convention. As the resolutions on abortion demonstrate, resolutions in general are too brief to begin to address the complexity of moral issues. Further, only canons passed by General Convention have binding character, and the status of resolutions addressing moral issues is not clear. Do they express "the mind of General Convention?" Are they advisory and, if so, what does that mean?

A more likely means of church teaching would be pastoral letters by bishops. I say this knowing how ineffective they can be, as, for example, was "A Theological Reflection Paper on Abortion" prepared by the Theology Committee of the House of Bishops and approved by the House of Bishops in 1984. Still, only such broader forms of address will enable bishops to teach. Bishops' letters can be formulated over a longer period of time and utilize resources in their composition unavailable to General Convention committees at the time of Convention. Pastoral letters by bishops, moreover, are an existing institution in the Episcopal Church. Presently they carry little weight because they have been written under most of the constraints which make resolutions of General Convention a poor means of teaching. But such constraints are avoidable, as pastoral letters recently published in the Roman Catholic Church in the United States have shown.[13]

The primary task of Episcopal pastoral letters would be to address fundamental issues in a way which would enable the moral formation of the whole church. Such documents would need to develop arguments which can persuade rather than simply appeal to the authority of the office of bishop or the institution of General Convention. In terms of abortion, these arguments would require addressing basic theological and moral issues. The need for this more capacious form is obvious when one begins to identify what some of these basic theological and moral issues are. For example, what is the theological and moral status of creaturely life? Is it sacred? If so, why? And what does sacredness mean in this context? In what sense is the theological language of sacredness different from the secular language of the dignity of human life?

Another basic question that teaching through pastoral letters could address is the meaning of bringing new life into the world for human beings in general and for Christians in particular. Both individually and communally, why can the *Book of Common Prayer* claim that "the birth of a child is a joyous and solemn occasion in the life of a family [and] . . . occasion for rejoicing in the Christian community"? That is, what theology of procreation, parenting, and nurturing of children does this imply? And what are the implications of this theology for the issue of elective abortion?

A final issue to be addressed is the theological and moral assessment of the "pro-choice" position in the current abortion debate. What is the good which is being protected and defended in the pro-choice position? What, if anything, in the Christian faith legitimates the good or value of self-determination and the control of a woman over her own powers of procreation?

Besides raising basic questions and issues, a teaching document must present informed judgments about answers to the questions and issues. This can be done without closing off discussion. But the church's moral education must offer positive teaching and not just define the field of debate. For example, I would argue that inherent in the structure of Christian love, agape, as a moral norm, is self-determination. Agape, as exemplified by God in Christ and commanded of us, is self-determination to be for another. Christians, therefore, must affirm self-determination as an essential human good because it is an essential aspect of the structure of acts of authentic Christian love. This point has obvious relevance to the good being protected and promoted by the pro-choice side of the current abortion debate.

On the other hand, the procreative power inherent in heterosexual intercourse is a great good in relation to society as such. Also, arguably, it is a means by which couples share and show forth, through their sexual powers, something of the generativity and creativity which classical theology ascribes to God as Trinity and as Creator, in whose image men and women are made. Further, beneath our ordinary self-awareness as agents who dispose over ourselves lies an even more fundamental awareness: we do not originate our lives or the lives of others, but we receive our existence as a gift. With this awareness of human life as a gift arises simultaneously the moral insight that human life is not simply at our disposal. This awareness may be the root of the natural moral law precept against the taking of innocent life. Moreover, ethicists have argued that bringing children into the world and nurturing them relates directly to Christian identity, since children evoke and require love from us. They are signs to the world that Christians have hope in the meaning of the human story. Thus, the very nature of Christian identity may create a bias toward the bearing, protecting, and nurturing of children.

Whether or not one agrees with these theological and moral views, they indicate the level of substantive doctrinal thought which must be engaged by any adequate church teaching on abortion. As positive proposals relevant to the issue of abortion, such teaching would provide a starting point for formation of conscience throughout the church. Issued by a group of bishops with other competent authors, such a study paper would not replace the work of others, but would promote moral dialogue, debate, and formation at parish, diocesan, provincial, and national levels of the church.

Roman Catholic pastoral letters on peace and on the economy provide models of what is needed in the Episcopal Church. Obviously, the Roman Catholic letters cannot serve as a model in every sense because the structure of teaching authority in the Roman Catholic Church is different from that in the Episcopal Church or in any branch of Anglicanism. But the identification of what issues are important and why, the linking of current teaching to the Christian tradition, the grounding of teaching in appropriate standards, and the identification of factors specific to the contemporary situation in which people live their lives—these elements in Roman Catholic pastoral letters can serve as a model for letters of teaching by bishops in the Episcopal Church.

Endnotes

1. For example, Timothy F. Sedgwick, "Responding to the Abortion Debate," *Saint Luke's Journal of Theology*, Vol. 30 (1987) 4:pp. 253–264, and David H. Smith, *Health and Medicine in the Anglican Tradition: Conscience, Community and Compromise* (New York: Crossroad, 1986), pp. 88–96.

2. For example, the Committee on Childbirth and Abortion, *Abortion: The Dialogue Continues. Pastoral and Educational*

Guidelines for Parish Use (Episcopal Diocese of Virginia, 1987).

3. *Journal of the General Convention*, 1967, pp. 308–309.

4. See appended copy of the 1967 Resolution.

5. See the discussion by Douglas B. Edwards, "Abortion: Does the Episcopal Church Have a Policy?", *The Living Church* (8 July 1984), pp. 8–9.

6. See the *Journal of the General Convention*, 1982, C-155.

7. See the *Journal of the General Convention*, 1985, pp. 509–510.

8. See *The Blue Book*, 1988, pp. 149–154.

9. Ibid., p. 153.

10. Beverly Wildung Harrison, *Our Right to Choose: Toward a New Ethic of Abortion* (Boston: Beacon Press, 1983).

11. See, for example, Katherine H. Ragsdale's critique in "The Episcopal Church and Abortion," *The Witness* (June 1989), pp. 17–20.

12. For one insightful Christian theological reflection on abortion see William Wepehowski, "The Pathos and Promise of Christian Ethics: A Study of the Abortion Debate," *Horizons*, Vol. 12 (1985) 2:pp. 284–310.

13. An example of a denominational study paper on abortion is the Presbyterian Church's *The Covenant of Life and the Caring Community and Covenant and Creation: Theological Reflection on Contraception and Abortion* (Office of the General Assembly, 1983). For a useful collection of official church statements on abortion with a good history of abortion legislation in the United States see J. Gordon Melton, ed., *The Church Speaks On Abortion. Official Statements from Religious Bodies and Ecumenical Organizations* (Detroit: Gale Research, 1989).

Position of the General Convention, 1982

Resolved, . . . That the following principles and guidelines adopted by the 65th General Convention (1976) and reaffirmed by the 66th General Convention (1979) be reaffirmed by this 67th General Convention:

1. The beginning of new human life, because it is a gift of the power of God's love for his people, and thereby sacred, should not and must not be undertaken unadvisedly or lightly but in

full accordance of the understanding for which this power to conceive and give birth is bestowed by God.

2. Such understanding includes the responsibility for Christians to limit the size of their families and to practice responsible birth control. Such means for moral limitations do not include abortion for convenience.

3. The position of this Church, stated at the 62nd General Convention of the Church in Seattle in 1967, which declared support for the "termination of pregnancy" particularly in those cases where "the physical or mental health of the mother is threatened seriously, or where there is substantial reason to believe that the child would be born badly deformed in mind or body, or where the pregnancy has resulted from rape or incest" is reaffirmed. Termination of pregnancy for these reasons is permissible.

4. In those cases where it is firmly and deeply believed by the person or persons concerned that pregnancy should be terminated for causes other than the above, members of this Church are urged to seek the advice and counsel of a Priest of this Church, and, where appropriate, penance.

5. Whenever members of this Church are consulted with regard to proposed termination of pregnancy, they are to explore, with the person or persons seeking advice and counsel, other preferable courses of action.

6. The Episcopal Church expresses its unequivocal opposition to any legislation on the part of the national or state governments which would abridge or deny the right of individuals to reach informed decisions in this matter and to act upon them.

The Journal of the General Convention, 1982, p. C–155-156

Position of the General Convention, 1988

RESOLVED, the House of Deputies concurring, That the 69th General Convention adopt the following statement on childbirth and abortion:

All human life is sacred. Hence, it is sacred from its inception until death. The Church takes seriously its obligation to help form the consciences of its members concerning this sacredness. Human life, therefore, should be initiated only advisedly and in full accord with this understanding of the power to conceive and give birth which is bestowed by God.

It is the responsibility of our congregations to assist their members in becoming informed concerning the spiritual, physiological and psychological aspects of sex and sexuality.

The *Book of Common Prayer* affirms that "the birth of a child is a joyous and solemn occasion in the life of a family. It is also an occasion for rejoicing in the Christian community." (p. 440) As Christians we also affirm responsible family planning.

We regard all abortion as having a tragic dimension, calling for the concern and compassion of all the Christian community.

While we acknowledge that in this country it is the legal right of every woman to have a medically safe abortion, as Christians we believe strongly that if this right is exercised, it should be used only in extreme situations. We emphatically oppose abortion as a means of birth control, family planning, sex selection, or any reason of mere convenience.

In those cases where an abortion is being considered, members of this Church are urged to seek the dictates of their consciences in prayer, to seek the advice and counsel of members of the Christian community and where appropriate the sacramental life of this Church.

Whenever members of this Church are consulted with regard to a problem pregnancy, they are to explore, with grave seriousness, with the person or persons seeking advice and counsel, as alternatives to abortion, other positive courses of action, including, but not limited to, the following possibilities: the parents raising the child; another family member raising the child; making the child available for adoption.

It is the responsibility of members of this Church, especially the clergy, to become aware of local agencies and resources which will assist those faced with problem pregnancies.

We believe that legislation concerning abortions will not address the root of the problem. We therefore express our deep conviction that any proposed legislation on the part of national or state governments regarding abortions must take special care to see that individual conscience is respected, and that the responsibility of individuals to reach informed decisions in this matter is acknowledged and honored.

The Journal of the General Convention, 1988, pp. 683-684

4

The Economic Order

Timothy F. Sedgwick

Introduction

The Episcopal Church has no clearly stated moral teachings addressing the economic order. What statements there are come from the two governing bodies of General Convention, the House of Deputies and the House of Bishops; from standing committees, commissions, and executive council and the professional staff of the national church as established by General Convention, and from the House of Bishops. This work is most often presented to an official church body and then published only in the official proceedings of General Convention. Even in the case of bishops' pastoral letters, such works are distributed to congregations and often made available to be read only once.

Whether reports, resolutions, or pastoral letters, teachings are generally short, more matters of moral declaration than broadly informed, reasoned arguments. As Robert Hood concluded in his study of *The Social Teachings in the Episcopal Church*, moral teachings tend to be episodic and reflect the "haste and shallowness with which the synods frequently deal with social issues."[1] This leads laity as well as clergy to discount what work is done by the national church. Teaching is, therefore, left to particular communities of faith whose attitudes and understandings may or may not be shaped by the work of dioceses and the national church. In this regard, the Episcopal Church may be among the most congregational of churches.

Teachings on the Economic Order

In the Episcopal Church moral understandings informing moral judgments regarding the economic order reflect three basic convictions: the absolute value of the individual, the communal character of human life, and freedom as essential to being human. Again and again these central convictions are expressed. Among the first statements was that from the Joint Commission on Relations of Capital and Labor created by the General Convention in 1901 and which reported to the next General Convention in 1904. Their mandate was itself an expression of these convictions. The commission's task was "to act as arbitrators, should their services be desired, between the men and their employers, with a view to bring about mutual conciliation and harmony in the spirit of the Prince of Peace."[2] In their first report they assessed that the cause of violence in relations between labor and management was fundamentally moral. The conflict resulted, they believed, from a lack of mutual trust—"the prejudice and passion" on one side and the "covetousness and the sins which proceed from the inordinate love of riches" on the other.[3] Given the infinite value of all people, the commission focused on those most vulnerable. In particular, it deplored "the employment of children in factories and mills." "Nothing," they said, "is so important in a human community as a human being."[4]

The dignity of the individual in community, according to the commission, is realized through free acts of sacrifice and service. This conviction continues to sound through the years in other statements on the economic order made by ECUSA. In 1913, for example, the General Convention emphasized the need for insuring that the needs of individuals were met so that they could participate in the larger community. In terms of "the ideal of social justice," the church "demands the achievement of a social order in which the social cause of poverty and the gross human waste of the present order shall be eliminated, and in which every worker shall have a just return for that which he produced, a free opportunity for self-development, and a fair share in all the gains of progress."[5] These conditions are to be brought about through the transformation of the will, resulting in actions of sacrifice and service. Social justice "can only be achieved," they said, "by [putting] the common welfare above private gain."[6] In 1922, the bishops again simply said that what is necessary is "cooperation in service for the common good in place of unrestricted competition for private or sectional advantage."[7]

In several pastoral letters the bishops spoke in more theological tones and claimed that the church is God's means of bringing the world into communion. In the General

Convention pastoral of 1916 they wrote:

> With the Incarnation as the corner-stone of the Faith, our common humanity contains in itself God's assurance that we have the capacity for universal brotherhood. God's executive agency for bringing in His Kingdom and His righteousness is the Church of Jesus Christ.[8]

In their 1919 pastoral from General Convention the bishops repeated this claim: "The Church is the one society of men in which God has covenanted with us to dwell. It is a social organism charged with the performance of a social task."[9] Through its laity, employers, and employees, the economic order may move toward "neighborliness, friendship, and brotherhood."[10]

In the midst of the Great Depression the church sounded a more somber note, but the basic vision of Christian faith in relationship to the economic order remained the same. In their annual meeting in 1933 in Davenport, Iowa, the House of Bishops addressed the collapse of the economic order. "Widespread suffering, hunger and distress in the face of unparalleled power, mechanical ingenuity and prodigal abundance present an appalling paradox such as our nation has never before witnessed. A selfish and soulless individualism . . . [has] wrought havoc in our social and economic life."[11]

The cross is then witnessed as a call to self-sacrifice for the sake of establishing a new economic order that will realize Christian ideals. "No standards," they said, "short of the Christian standards can lead us out of our darkness into light. No ideal save that of the Kingdom of God can satisfy the minds and hearts of Christian people."[12]

> No mere reestablishment of an old economic order will suffice. Christ demands a new order in which there shall be a more equitable distribution of material wealth, more certain assurance of security for the unemployed and aged, and, above all else, an order which shall substitute the motive of service for the motive of gain. . . . For us the Cross stands as the symbol of a world recovery act. It demands that we become world recovery agents who dare to carry the Cross.[13]

In terms of particular proposals regarding the economic order, the national church documents spoke of the need to provide a wage sufficient to meet basic human needs, to insure that labor has some voice in the decisions of management, and to have collective bargaining in which arbitration was the rule, rather than strikes and lockouts. These points were stated, for example, in resolutions passed at the 1922 General Convention. In addition to "minimum subsistence wages," there should be "a comfort and saving wage." In terms of what was called industrial democracy, the resolution affirmed that workers should have "some voice in the control of industry." Specifically, collective bargaining was affirmed with the understanding that this "must take the place of the ruinous strife of strikes."[14]

Despite the rise of totalitarian rule—first in the rise of Hitler and then following World War II in the rise of communism—bishops' pastorals and reports to General Convention continued to view Christianity in terms of the value of the individual fulfilled in a community of service. Discussion of economic life and order focused on reconstruction following the war. Emphasis was given to providing support for a new order and world community, rather than seeking retribution abroad and individual prosperity at home. Perhaps the most constructive work at the national level was done by the Joint Commission on Reconstruction. From the 1940s to the 1950s this commission convened regional meetings and solicited papers in order to elicit a broader public conversation, both in the church and in society-at-large. Seeking to avoid "vague generalizations and aspirations," they requested papers which reflected different viewpoints on issues ranging from communism and the world order to the use of atomic energy.[15] Penguin Press published a first collection of papers in 1946. This Penguin paperback, *Christianity Takes a Stand*, sold 50,000 copies, and a second volume, *The Christian Demand for Social Justice* (New American Library), was published in 1949.

In terms of a moral and theological perspective on the economic order, however, the only significant change was in the addressing of issues of power. Previously, the church had seen change in the economic order arising from a change of will, the development of trust, and acts of self-sacrifice. Slowly the church came to the conclusion that economic justice—equal participation of all in the economic life of the society—could only be achieved through the redistribution of power to the disadvantaged. This change was evidenced in the response to the call of Black leaders for "Black Power." The initial successes of the civil rights movement in the 1960s addressed legalized forms of racism in the United States—for example, the segregation of public facilities such as public transportation, restaurants, schools, and universities. The intractable character of racism was, however, evident in the institutionalization of power in the country's education, economic, and political systems. In order to make participation and self-determination possible in American society, changes were necessary in housing, education, job opportunities, business investments, corporate decisions, and political programs. These changes required a sharing of economic and political power.

Highlighting this change in perspective, Presiding Bishop John Hines, in his General Convention sermon in 1967, called for "the appropriation of substantial sums of money to community organizations involved in the betterment of depressed urban areas, and under the control of those who are largely both black and poor, that their power for self-determination may be increased and their dignity restored."[16] In response to this sermon, both houses of the General Convention approved an "open letter" confirming a policy enabling the poor, especially the ghetto-poor, to gain an effective voice and visible presence in the decisions which affect their own lives." "We want," the letter continued, "Episcopal Church money invested to make this process work." "The new and crucial principle" governing such investment was to be that "we should budget some of our money for others to spend on priorities they themselves have set."[17] The Convention proceeded to fund what was called the General Convention Special Programs for "enablement projects." While focused on Black self-determination, grants were also given to Native American and Hispanic projects.[18]

In opposition to funding directly community groups independent of the church, some parishes and dioceses began withholding funds to the national church. General Convention and the national church, though, continued to view economic justice as requiring more than mutual trust and cooperation. As the "open letter" in response to Presiding Bishop Hines said, "We know that the 'have-nots' must share in the power of the 'haves' before common community can be open to either."[19] The idealism of earlier statements, though, remained. Sharing of power and the forming of a common community may come through commitment and self-sacrifice.

Pastoral from the Urban Bishops' Coalition

Perhaps the document most representative of the church's evolving understanding of economic life and order is the 1987 report from the Urban Bishops' Coalition, "Economic Justice and the Christian Conscience."[20] This document was presented to the fall meeting of the House of Bishops, who voted to "commend it to the widest possible range of membership in the Episcopal Church for study, reflection and response."[21] Following the meeting of bishops, 82 bishops representing 67 of the 120 dioceses in the United States personally endorsed the document. While still only about one-fifth the length of the Roman Catholic pastoral on the economy approved by the National Conference of Catholic Bishops a year earlier,[22] this twenty-five-page document written in the form of a pastoral letter is the most extensive document addressing Christian faith and the economic order received and commended by the House of Bishops.

In content, "Economic Justice and the Christian Conscience" reflects previous moral teachings, occasional as they may be, with continued emphasis on the dignity of the individual, the communal nature of human life and fulfillment, and the freedom of the individual. Christian faith continues to be understood in terms of the transformation of individuals from private concerns for individual security to service and participation in the community. The need to insure that the poor have sufficient power for self-determination and for participation in the society-at-large is evident. Despite the stark picture of the disparity between rich and poor, in the end the vision remains liberal and optimistic in its belief that through conversion and self-sacrifice humans can realize the ideals of Christian faith. At the least, conflict and tragedy seldom come into view.

The pastoral letter begins with what Roman Catholic teachings have referred to as signs of the times, the events in the world which call Christians to respond. Now, more than ever before, we are confronted by the paradox of increased prosperity for many in the midst of others who live in the grip of poverty. This economic order is fragile; unless the widening gap between rich and poor is overcome, the economic order will collapse. What is needed is deliverance "from the idolatry of false priorities and irresponsible behavior."[23] Basic human needs must be met, including food, shelter, medical care, the freedom of self-determination, and the education and opportunity to participate in the economic life of society. For Christians "these elemental human priorities" are "underlined" by Jesus' call to feed the hungry, house the homeless, clothe the naked, tend to the sick, and let the oppressed go free (Mt. 25, Lk. 4:18)[p.2].

The catalogue of statistics presented is daunting. In the United States one out of seven people is poor, with poverty rates for Blacks and Hispanics at almost one in three.

> Between 1979 and 1984, a total of 11.5 million workers were displaced—nearly half of these having been on the job for three years or more and 5.1 million of whom were still out of work in 1985. . . . Moreover, among the 9 million new jobs created, two out of three are unfortunately in the lowest paying sectors of the U.S. economy—retail trade and health. In the former category the average weekly wage for the newly employed over the last seven years is $174—well below the government established poverty line ($215.44 weekly for a family of four). [p.4]

The number of those unable to afford medical care has increased from twenty-five to thirty-seven million; less than fifty percent of people living below the poverty line have any access to medical services. Perhaps the most stark sign of poverty are the homeless people, who now number between two and three million. Many of them enmeshed in alcohol and drug abuse, the homeless constitute "a vast new underclass of poor." (pp. 5–6)

The economic pastoral goes on to read the signs of the times from a global perspective. The poverty in the United States is dwarfed by the "more than 800 million people in Third World countries [who] live in absolute poverty." The exploitation of foreign labor through poverty-level wages and the indebtedness of foreign countries make it nearly impossible for the countries themselves to address the problems of poverty. In turn, public and private debt in the United States, captivity to the arms race, the sluggish growth of labor productivity, the stagnation of real wages, and the increase of inflationary pressures limit the ability of the United States to address these global needs. (pp. 6–7)

In the midst of the "very complex, world-wide system of interrelationships" that form economic life, the Christian is not to seek specific policies first, but rather to raise consciousness of injustice in light of the Christian vision of fulfillment.

In sketching a theological vision, people are created for community. Fulfillment is not individual. All persons are stewards, to care for and enter into communion with those beyond themselves. Given this vision, private ownership of land is never ultimate but is given only for the sake of the common good (Lev. 25:23).

Jesus incarnates this theological vision of human life. Time and again Jesus makes it abundantly clear that all economic arrangements must serve to strengthen the common life of people, rather than to serve as a dominating force over their lives. His vision for all men and women is that God intends them for community. And he established a beloved community, the Church, largely to be the sign and co-sign for all human community. Productivity, in his view, is only a means, even if an important means, to this larger end. Thus any social pattern which substitutes productivity or the consumption of things or personal enrichment or even survival for a creative, loving relationship with God and one's neighbor in community becomes idolatrous, sinful. (p. 10)

Reflecting earlier teachings, Christian faith is viewed in this pastoral as a matter of the deliverance of the will from bondage, a transformation of the will in the love of God and neighbor. Perhaps the greatest obstacle to this conversion is the yearning for security: the pastoral notes that "for the Israelites in the wilderness freedom was in fact so worrisome that many began to yearn for the security of the slavery back in Egypt." Similarly, "those in the seats of power in our affluent society will have great trouble giving up on the unjust systems and arrangements that characterize our society even though we know they are enslaving us along with the poor." (p. 10) For the Urban Bishops' Coalition, the task before the church is the transformation of the will in order to reform "our human priorities, societal assumptions, ideas, cultural mores, and 'habits of the heart' " (p. 11).

In terms of specific proposals, the pastoral supports experiments to insure the opportunity for participation in the economic order. Suggested are "cooperatives, community corporations, worker-owned firms and local, regional and national economic planning." The pastoral goes on to emphasize that beyond addressing the consequences of poverty at the personal level—for example, through soup kitchens, overnight shelters, and counseling programs—the church must stress that for most people poverty is not the result of "personal mistakes or some lack of personal ambition." Above all, poverty occurs because of the "happenstances of birth, by lack of education and training opportunity, or by economic decisions made by others which curtail or eliminate the job in which they had invested their lives." (p. 13) Given that the United States ranks twenty-seventh among 124 nations in matters of welfare, literacy and education, health care, and housing, the Urban Bishops' Coalition could only conclude that failure in these areas is a matter of a lack of will to "narrow the gap between the rich and the poor." The transformation of will, moreover, will "take long term witness." (p. 14)

Finally, "Economic Justice and Christian Conscience" identifies two areas of importance for the transformation necessary to address poverty. First, the church "has a special obligation to give the Christian theology of work a higher priority" than it has in recent years. Work has too often been reduced to a commodity, not only by management but by labor as well. Such a narrow conception of work results in an adversarial relationship between management and labor and makes difficult the development of broader forms of participation. In contrast, says the pastoral, "work is the stage on which we daily re-enact our ability to master circumstance and fate, where we achieve distinction and receive recognition, and where we socialize and act together towards common goals." (p. 14)

Second, the transformation called for requires government action. Government must do for the citizens as a whole what cannot be done by individuals or corporate bodies with more particular responsibilities. The pastoral steers away from endorsing specific programs, such as how to finance national health care, how to insure adequate child care, or how to create more jobs providing a living wage. The pastoral is clear, however, regarding policy. Government must assume responsibility to insure basic human welfare, education and training, housing, health care, safety and sanitation, and the opportunity for employment. (pp. 15–17)

The Urban Bishops' Coalition concludes by again stating that "our economic problems persist not so much because of fiscal imponderables as because we lack the moral will as a people to reorder our value priorities." Community in which the dignity of the individual is preserved through equality and participation in the economic order "requires rebuilding a new relationship between capital and community, between those who make significant economic decisions and those who must live with the consequences of those decisions." (p. 17) Signs of hope are found in the tremendous resources available in the United States—for example, a high level of technological expertise, an educated and well-trained labor force, and extensive natural resources. Other signs are noted in new experiments of cooperation—private corporations working with public officials to improve public education, community-based credit unions uniting business and neighborhood, community/worker owned enterprises, and communities and workers working with industry to modernize and produce new products. (p. 18)

The pastoral warns, however, that now is a time of crisis. Failure to respond to the signs of poverty in order to create a just community will result in "a worldwide banking debacle, a major depression, riots, war, or a combination of all four" (p. 19). In its concluding sentence, the pastoral ends by emphasizing that a much more critical exploration of justice issues than has ever before been imagined in the church "is a necessary prelude to the ultimate work of clarifying for our society the positive goals needed for a new day and the longer term strategies for achieving them" (p. 20).

Adequacy of Moral Teachings

These moral teachings on economic life and order consistently give expression to a form of moral idealism. Christian faith is identified with an ideal state of affairs for human life in history. Redemption is understood in terms of the realization of this ideal. The transformation of the human will is at the heart of this vision. In faith idolatry is broken. Security is not to be found in self-sufficiency. Faith shows that people are fulfilled only as they become members of a community that embraces all people. With this knowledge of heart and mind comes a change in priorities reflected in service and self-sacrifice, mutual trust and love. While economic power is necessary for participation in the life of the community, as the Davenport pastoral evidences, the cross itself is a symbol of self-sacrifice and service that remains the basis and the promise of the realization of a new order.

In terms of the church and society, the moral idealism of the church's teaching is reflected in a Christendom model in which the church is the soul of the nation. As the soul of the nation, the church is to be its conscience and the vanguard in effecting social change. The 1916 bishops' pastoral spoke of the church as "God's executive agency for bringing in His Kingdom and His righteousness."[24] The report in 1966 from the Committee on the Office of a Bishop went so far as to claim that the primary task of the bishop was in the area of "public ministries." This "means that a Diocese through and with the Bishop, seeks to be the agent and enabler of social change in community policy affecting basic issues of community life."[25]

Both the content and the occasional character of these moral teachings raise significant questions for bishops and for the church regarding the exercise of their teaching responsibilities. In particular, the hasty and episodic nature of these statements seems to ensure their failure to provide moral reasoning that illumines the conflict of goods that must be addressed and adjudicated in public policy. The church's teaching, therefore, fails to provide an adequate framework to inform practical moral judgments and public policy debate. In view of the dominant liberal perspective of moral idealism, policy proposals are advanced. While the proposals may parade as moral teachings, they are in fact statements of advocacy.

In contrast to the Episcopal Church and Protestant ethics in general, the Roman Catholic Church has a tradition of moral teachings which identifies moral conflicts and provides guidance without determining policy. For example, Roman Catholic moralists have sought guidance in addressing the good of society when in tension with individual liberty in terms of "the principle of subsidiarity":

> Just as it is gravely wrong to take from individuals what they can accomplish by their own initiative and industry and give it to the community, so also it is an injustice and at the same time a grave evil and disturbance of right order to assign to a greater and higher association what lesser and subordinate organizations can do. For every social activity ought of its very nature to furnish help (*subsidium*) to the member of the body social, and never destroy or absorb them.[26]

In addition to the principle of subsidiarity, principles of justice have also been articulated. Most recently expressed in *Economic Justice for All*, justice is understood in light of the larger Christian perspective of God's justice, of right relationship, in which all persons share in a community "marked by the fullness of love, compassion, holiness and peace" (par. 68). The basic justice of such a community is a matter of "the establishment of minimum levels of participation in the life of the human community for all persons" (par. 77). This understanding of a just society may be described and guidance gained by developing the terms of justice—commutative justice, distributive justice, and social justice.

Commutative justice calls for fundamental fairness in all agreements and exchanges between individuals and private social groups. . . . Distributive justice requires that the allocation of income, wealth and power in society be evaluated in light of its effects on persons whose basic material needs are unmet. . . . Social justice implies that persons have an obligation to be active and productive participants in the life of society and that society has a duty to enable them to participate in this way. (pars. 69, 70, 71)

Again, moral principles do not in themselves solve the questions of what ought to be done, but they identify the moral conflict and thereby provide guidance in terms of what goods must be addressed. For example, the Roman bishops' pastoral moves back and forth between the call for basic justice without which there is "a threat to the solidarity of the human community" (par. 74), and a concern to honor the freedom and dignity of the individual. In contrast to Roman Catholic teachings, teachings in the Episcopal Church lack the articulation of moral principles. Therefore, instead of illumining the conflicts which must be confronted in light of the fundamental Christian concern for justice, the teachings are, at best, reduced to prophetic outcries. At worst, the pronouncements of the church are ideological resolutions in which Christian faith is confused with particular policies and programs.

This identification of Christian faith with particular policies and programs is compounded by the failure to offer detailed analyses of specific problems. The specific proposals most often advanced by the church include expansion and reform of income supports, a broadening as well as an improvement in public-sector delivery of human services, the creation of public service jobs, national health insurance, increase in minimum wage, new tax revenues, and major cuts in wasteful military spending.[27] These proposals are made without consideration of the range of policy options and possible courses of action and consequences. Prescriptions are, therefore, abstracted from a concrete understanding of actual choices. When combined with the lack of moral understandings and principles to inform the moral issues involved, it should not be surprising when the voice of the church is dismissed as ill-informed and naive by those whom the church most wants to listen.

Perhaps most significantly, the lack of moral reasoning and detailed analysis reflects the inadequate moral idealism that is assumed theologically. The moral idealism of the church's teachings assumes that the ideals of individual dignity, universal community, and human freedom complement one another and may be realized in history. All that is required is the transformation of the will. Given the Christian vision and the experience of these ideals in the Christian community, the individual is freed from idolatry for the sake of a community of service. Here, basically, is the liberalism of the American social gospel in which the essence of Christianity was expressed in the then-inclusive language of "the Fatherhood of God and the brotherhood of man." As the events of the twentieth century evidenced to theological critics of liberalism, this stance is inadequate and naive. For example, moral idealism assumes a univocal biblical theology in which human fulfillment is the ultimate end of God. Such a view is inadequate in comprehending the diversity of witnesses in scripture,[28] our understanding of human history, and our own experience as well. And nothing, I believe, is further from the truth of the gospel.

Grace is never a means of realizing moral ideals. Instead, as suggested by the parables, grace is more a matter of the conversion of heart and mind. Those in need are not objects of charity who present the obstacles that must be overcome in order to realize the community of fulfillment promised in scripture. The poor are among the strangers through whom God is present; they invite us beyond ourselves by challenging our complacent security, preoccupations, defensiveness, and self-righteousness. They effect our conversion, the enlargement of the soul, by bringing us into a broader and deeper relationship with God.[29]

From this perspective, the Christian life is not a matter of moral ideals working themselves out in history or reaching fulfillment beyond history. Rather, at the heart of Christian faith is the experience of grace, of the gratuitousness of life itself. Luther expressed this in terms of justification by grace, while Richard Hooker spoke in terms of humans having as their distinctive end "being rapt with the love of [God's] beauty" and thereby participating in the works of God.[30]

In contrast to moral idealism, the refusal to tie grace to human fulfillment in the realization of moral ideals raises fundamental questions about human possibilities and about the role and limits of government. H. Richard Niebuhr, for example, described how in the development of the United States the desire for limiting the exercise of the power of government and the structuring of balances of power in government was, at least in part, formed out of the deep conviction that God alone is sovereign.[31] In this light, the perennial problem of human life and government is the abuse of power for private gain. In order to serve the common good, government must disperse power to prevent its concentration in any one place, whether public government or private corporations.[32]

With this shift to a theology of grace not dependent upon the realization of an ideal state of affairs in history comes an equivalent shift in understanding of the church. Instead of vanguard, the church is witness and sacrament. Instead of the primary concern of the church being social change, the church must focus on what it means and what is required in order to be a faithful community. Moral teachings are not first of all directed to society but to the church itself, in order that the community can bear witness to the grace of God it has known through Jesus Christ: quite simply, to be a sign of that grace through its own life.[33]

Whether this shift in theological understanding is thought to be more adequate or not, what is most noteworthy regarding the teachings of the Episcopal Church is that there is no critical reflection on the central understandings of Christian faith and the task of the church. In fact, the governing vision is assumed rather than developed and argued in terms of scripture, tradition, and other understandings of the world. Bishops' pastorals, resolutions, and other actions of General Convention—including the work of interim bodies such as commissions, standing committees, executive council, and the professional staff at the national church offices—provide reflections which appear to remain culturally captive to a theological liberalism that was dominant in the nineteenth and early twentieth centuries.

Challenges to the Development of Moral Teachings

While this particular assessment of the theology assumed in the statements of the Episcopal Church on economic life and order may be debated, the lack of moral teachings adequate for identifying outstanding moral issues and for informing actual policy choices is indisputable. Instead of informing conscience and public debate in general, the void created by the lack of such teachings is filled by particular advocates. The church becomes a battleground between adversaries. Amidst strident voices and demands, the councils of the church—from the delegations to General Convention to membership on committees and commissions—are formed to ensure representation of particular constituencies and interests. In this setting the development of well-informed teachings is nearly impossible. The increasingly adversarial politics of the church is, of course, not limited to moral teachings. Beyond issues of human sexuality, abortion, or social justice, divisiveness extends to all areas of life in the church—from liturgical reform to interpretations of scripture, from women's ordination to the meaning of the resurrection.

In order to address the problems of teaching and discipline amidst conflicting stances, in 1967 Presiding Bishop John Hines appointed an Advisory Committee on Theological Freedom and Social Responsibility. The work of the committee was formed in specific response to the continuing tensions resulting from Bishop James Pike's views on a range of theological matters—including the virgin birth, the incarnation, and the Trinity. Some bishops had called for an ecclesiastical trial on heresy. Others supported Pike, at least his right to explore and question orthodoxy without condemnation. A majority of bishops voted to censure him. In response to the "Pike Affair" and the issues of teaching, authority, and discipline, the committee saw the fundamental need to be the development of structures and opportunities for teaching and education. The committee specifically recommended educational opportunities for clergy and laity; continuing education for clergy; corporate study and reflection for bishops, including regular communication with theologians and other persons with particular expertise; and the establishment of a Standing Commission on the Church's Teaching.[34]

The development of such teaching and educational opportunities will not eliminate divergent views and the question of what are the boundaries that constitute Christian belief and practice. Teaching alone cannot replace the need for discipline. What such teaching can do, however, is constitute a ground of common convictions and understandings that will not narrowly define Christian faith in terms of particular concerns and convictions. The need for developing teaching materials and educational opportunities is, if anything, even greater now than twenty-five years ago. Specific reforms are needed.

Given their particular responsibility "to guard the faith, unity, and discipline of the Church" through their episcopal oversight, bishops bear the burden of initiating the reforms necessary to make the teaching ministry of the church more effective. As the 1967 report recommends, the House of Bishops needs corporate study and discussion in conversations with the theologians of the church and others with particular expertise. In terms of specific structures, committees and commissions must be organized with sufficient resources to address particular issues. In turn, the organization and work of the professional staff of the national church must support such work, rather than forming a bureaucracy that initiates its own programs to meet the needs and gain the support of a particular constituency to the exclusion of the broader tasks of teaching and education.

In developing pastoral letters on peace and on the economy, the National Conference of Catholic Bishops for the Roman Catholic Church in the United States provides one model for the organization and deployment of resources that have effectively created teachings and educational material. The Church of England has also organized its resources for teaching more successfully than the Episcopal Church. This is reflected, for example, in the work of its Board for Social Responsibility and its Doctrine Commission.[35] Both the National Conference of Catholic Bishops and the Church of England focused on particular issues and provided adequate time and budget for study and discussion, including consultation with theologians of the church, with others having professional knowledge, and with persons who had divergent points of view. They both also provided for the publication of materials. For the Roman Catholics this included broad publication of initial drafts of their pastoral letters. They then provided opportunities for study, discussion, and response to these drafts by theologians, clergy, and laity. Finally, other secondary materials were written to enable the critical engagement of the final documents in congregations, secondary schools, and colleges and universities.

As this study of the Episcopal Church and its moral teachings on the economic order evidences, the church has failed to develop anything more than occasional, ad hoc statements about economic life and order. These statements are not informed by any critical assessment and themselves lack the development of an ethical framework, including the moral principles that aid in understanding the conflict of moral goods which Christians struggle to honor and adjudicate. Failure to address in detail specific policies and problems, moreover, results in broad generalizations that inform neither individual conscience nor public policy decisions. Attempts to be specific are achieved only by taking ideological stances that ignore the complexity of public policy issues, including the trade-offs that are involved in adopting any specific program. New materials are not developed in reference to earlier work. They stand alone, pronounced but never promulgated.

The problems of developing teaching in the Episcopal Church are long-standing, now structurally endemic to the church. There are no remedial actions sufficient to effect the changes needed. In bearing the authority "to guard the faith, unity, and discipline of the Church," only the bishops can develop the structure and resources necessary for an effective teaching office and ministry in the church. This will require concerted and sustained attention and effort. Failure threatens the very capacity of the church to sustain its identity amidst adversarial politics. Persons will identify Christian faith with particular positions or, rejecting particular positions altogether, will withdraw from the concerns which incarnate faith in the world. Either response results not only in a crisis for the church in its own life, but, more fundamentally, in the capacity of the church to proclaim and bear witness to Christian faith itself.

Endnotes

1. Robert E. Hood, *Social Teachings in the Episcopal Church* (Harrisburg, PA: Morehouse Publishing, 1990), p. xix.

2. *Journal of the General Convention*, 1904, p. 530.

3. Ibid., p. 531.

4. Ibid., p. 532.

5. *Journal of the General Convention*, 1913, p. 122.

6. Ibid.

7. *Journal of the General Convention*, 1922, p. 543.

8. *Journal of the General Convention*, 1916, p. 403.

9. *Journal of the General Convention*, 1919, p. 507.

10. Ibid., p. 508.

11. *Journal of the General Convention*, 1943, p. 79.

12. Ibid.

13. Ibid., p. 80.

14. *Journal of the General Convention*, 1922, p. 378.

15. *Journal of the General Convention*, 1946, p. 586.

16. *Journal of the General Convention*, 1967, p. 2.

17. Ibid., p. 304.

18. See John Booty, *The Episcopal Church in Crisis* (Cambridge: Cowley Publications, 1988), pp. 60–65.

19. *Journal of the General Convention*, 1967, p. 305.

20. Urban Bishops' Coalition, "Economic Justice and the Christian Conscience" in *What Should We Value? A Theological and Economic Critique of "Economic Justice and the Christian Conscience"* (Sewanee: The Cumberland Center for Justice and Peace, 1989), Appendix, pp. 1–25.

21. *Journal of the General Convention*, 1988, p. 415. Indicative of the problem of promulgation, despite this commendation the document was not published as part of the proceedings from the 1987 meeting of the House of Bishops or in any other publication from the national church.

22. National Conference of Catholic Bishops, *Economic Justice for All: Catholic Social Teaching and the U.S. Economy* in *Origins*, Vol. 16 (27 November 1986) 24: pp. 409–455.

23. "Economic Justice and the Christian Conscience," Appendix, p. 1. Subsequent page references to this document are indicated in parentheses in the text.

24. *Journal of the General Convention*, 1916, p. 403.

25. *Journal of the General Convention*, 1967, Supplement B, p. 35.

26. *Economic Justice for All*, par. 99, quoted from *Quadragesimo Anno (On Reconstructing the Social Order)*, par. 79, published in *The Church and the Reconstruction of*

the *Modern World: The Social Encyclicals of Pius XI*, Terence P. McLaughlin, ed. (Garden City: Image, 1957), p. 247. Subsequent quotations from *Economic Justice for All* are indicated in the text in parentheses.

27. "Economic Justice and the Christian Conscience," p. 16.

28. See Brevard Childs, *Biblical Theology in Crisis* (Philadelphia: Westminster, 1970).

29. For the development of this perspective see Timothy F. Sedgwick, "Graceless Poverty and the Poverty of Grace," *Prophetic Visions and Economic Realities*, Charles R. Strain, ed. (Grand Rapids: Eerdmans, 1989), pp. 146–155.

30. Richard Hooker, *Of the Laws of Ecclesiastical Polity*, Arthur Stephen McGrade, ed. (New York: Cambridge University Press, 1989), Book I, chapter 4, section 1.

31. H. Richard Niebuhr, *The Kingdom of God in America* (New York: Harper & Row, 1938), pp. 75–87.

32. Reinhold Niebuhr continues to provide this critical perspective on the relationship between Christian faith and the social order. See, for example, *Moral Man and Immoral Society* (New York: Charles Scribner's Sons, 1932). For an application of a Niebuhrian perspective to the economy see Robert Benne, *The Ethic of Democratic Capitalism* (Philadelphia: Fortress, 1981).

33. Primary among those reflecting this shift in perspective is Stanley Hauerwas. See, for example, Stanley Hauerwas and William H. Willimon, *Resident Aliens: Life in the Christian Colony* (Nashville: Abingdon, 1989).

34. The *Journal of the General Convention*, 1967, Appendix 6.1–22.

35. See, for example, Church of England Board for Social Responsibility, *Marriage and the Family in Britain Today* (London: Church Information Office, 1974); *Prisons and Prisoners in England Today* (London: Church Information Office, 1978); *Homosexual Relationships* (London: Church Information Office, 1979); *The Church of England and Politics* (Cowley, Oxford: Bocardo & Church Army Press, 1980); *Housing and the Homeless* (London: Church Information Office, 1982). Two more limited examples of developing moral teachings are the Lutheran Church in America's work on homosexuality, *A Study of Issues Concerning Homosexuality* (Division of Missions, 1986; available from the

Evangelical Lutheran Church in America, 8765 W. Higgins
Road, Chicago, IL 60631), and the study of nuclear deterrence
by the Episcopal Diocese of Washington, *The Nuclear
Dilemma: A Christian Search for Understanding* (Cincinnati:
Forward Movement, 1987).

5

On War, Peace
and the Use of Force

Allan M. Parrent

The Episcopal Church, through its General Convention and House of Bishops, has issued numerous statements, resolutions, and pastoral letters on issues of war and peace. A pamphlet of the Episcopal Peace Fellowship, *Cross Before Flag*, contains excerpts from a number of such statements, beginning with a General Convention resolution of 1916.[1] Some of the works are of a general nature dealing briefly with the Christian understanding of war and participation in it. Others address specific issues such as nuclear freeze or the level of defense spending. In the post-1945 nuclear age, major concerns of statements from the church have included the nature of war in a nuclear age, the capabilities of nuclear weapons, and the impact of these on the Christian moral assessment of modern war and weaponry. The House of Bishops expressed this concern concisely in their 1982 pastoral letter: "Your bishops perceive the nuclear arms race as the most compelling issue in the world public order."[2]

The general purposes of this essay are to survey the major official statements of the Episcopal Church on war and peace in the decade of 1979–1988, to analyze and evaluate these statements in light of the justifiable war tradition to which historically the church has primarily adhered, and to examine both the coherence of the argumentation and the moral implications of the positions taken. The essay will then recommend some elements for the church to consider as it continues to address the perennial moral questions of war and the use of force in a Christian perspective, suggesting in the process some areas that need more careful and rigorous theological and ethical attention. The essay is in part the result of my own experience as a member of the Episcopal Church's Joint (later Standing) Commission on Peace from its inception in 1979 until 1988.

Beginning Stance of the 1962 Bishops' Pastoral

In 1979 the 66th General Convention voted to establish a Joint Commission on Peace, a body which became a standing commission in 1985. The commission was mandated to present to the 67th General Convention in 1982 a comprehensive program for implementing the 1962 House of Bishops' pastoral letter, a letter which had declared, "Because of the nature of the Christian faith, Christians have an imperative obligation to pray and work for peace among men and nations."[3] The 1962 pastoral letter was clearly intended to be the basis for the work of the Joint Commission as it sought to give some structure and content to the "imperative obligation" that Christians have. It established a theological basis and a set of specific Christian actions, both individual and corporate, which, while not quoted further in the 1979 resolution, were supposed to provide a general framework for the commission.

The 1962 pastoral letter recognized "confusion about the Christian's approach to the waging of war" in a nuclear age. It then affirmed "an approach of Christian realism which is grounded in the basic truths of the Christian gospel."[4] The theological basis for this pastoral letter was itself a classic summary of the approach of Christian realism. The pastoral called political leaders "to exercise the strongest discipline of conscience to prevent total war." All-out modern war, they said, cannot serve the purpose that war may once have served in securing justice and peace. Christians must seek to insure "that any war which breaks out anywhere in the world is limited. In any armed conflict, we must set clearly defined objectives and cease to wage war when they are achieved." Such judgments seem clearly to be based on the acceptance and application of the traditional just war criteria.[5]

The 1962 pastoral letter goes on to say, in the same vein of "Christian realism," that, given the social sin inherent in the world, the United States must remain strong militarily. With specific reference to nuclear deterrence it states:

> The Church recognizes that a strong military posture does serve as a deterrent to an aggressor nation intent upon military conflict. To this end, the Church further recognizes that the government must keep itself abreast of all developments in warfare. However, the Church declares that the concept of massive retaliation marked by obliteration bombing of large areas and masses of people should be repudiated.

That statement put the church on record as accepting, albeit reluctantly and soberly, a policy of nuclear deterrence. In keeping with the just war tradition, however, it placed that acceptance in the context of the justice in war (*jus in bello*) principle of discrimination—what is referred to as noncombatant immunity—as well as the related requirement that the government keep up with developments in weaponry that might make such discrimination more possible should deterrence fail.

The position of the Episcopal Church, according to this pastoral letter of 1962, might be summarized as follows:

1. A policy of nuclear deterrence is morally acceptable as a means of preventing war.

2. Obliteration bombing of population centers is morally unacceptable, both as the intention of a deterrent policy and as a military strategy should deterrence fail.

3. The only kind of war that might be morally acceptable would be one using limited means of force and having limited objectives.

4. Governments have a moral responsibility to continue research and development in weaponry in order to have weapons with the capabilities necessary for that kind of limited and discriminating use if deterrence should fail. Unless this is done the only deterrent available would be unacceptable on moral grounds and would also be an ineffective deterrent because the threat of the actual use of such a deterrent would not be credible.

Conflicting Directions of Bishops and Conventions

In spite of the 1962 pastoral letter, which the 1979 Convention mandated to be the basis for the work of the new peace commission, the resolutions of the 1979 Convention itself moved in other directions. First, it adopted as its own the resolution on "War and Violence" passed at the 1978 Lambeth Conference. That resolution included the statement, previously affirmed by several Lambeth Conferences and General Convention, that "war as a method of settling international disputes is incompatible with the teaching and example of our Lord Jesus Christ." Second, it passed a resolution that quoted the above statement once again, noted that conscription is used to raise armies to wage war, and on that basis opposed "peacetime conscription or any form of compulsory national service unless a national emergency is declared by the Congress."[6] An obvious question is what these resolutions are intended to mean in terms of Christian attitudes and actions. On the surface at least, the first seems to lead logically to pacifism, though that implication has never been explicitly stated. The second, which begins with the same premise, seems to find conscription morally questionable, yet indicates that a national emergency would nullify its morally questionable nature. Such resolutions give conflicting or unclear directions to church members and illustrate the need for moral clarity in church statements.

The conflict in teaching between the 1962 pastoral and the resolutions in 1979 was furthered by the 1981 pastoral letter of the House of Bishops entitled "Apocalypse and Hope." The bishops declared that "never before has it been so clear that reason forbids the use of violence, or the threat of it, as a means of securing one society against another."[7] The letter goes on to state, in an unusual juxtaposition of sentences, "The Christian tradition does not understand peace in the world to mean the absence of conflict. It means instead the abandonment of violence as a way of resolving even the most severe differences." Finally, the letter appeals to national leaders to "repudiate reliance on military threats in favor of the more demanding discipline of military restraint and negotiation for arms control."

The 1981 pastoral letter is confusing in part because of its failure to distinguish between violence and force. Violence is traditionally understood as the illegitimate and/or indiscriminate use of physical power, such as terrorist attacks on the innocent. In contrast, force is the discriminate use of physical power by those who have a legitimate grant of power, for example, the police or armies which act on behalf of governments, in order to uphold morally and legally valid goods and purposes. The pastoral letter seems, however, to equate force and violence and to reject the use of either by nations, or at least by Christians who are citizens of nations, as a means of securing a society. What the letter calls "the Christian tradition" is inadequately presented, since that tradition surely has room for making a moral distinction between, for example, terrorism and the measured use of legitimate force. Indeed, making such moral distinctions is one of the tasks of Christian ethics.

More specifically, in calling for "the abandonment of violence as a way of resolving even the most severe differences,"
the bishops' letter appears to be a call to vocational pacifism.
Such a conviction is a viable, morally defensible, and
demanding understanding of Christian faith. While individuals may legitimately choose such a calling, however, governments may not. Furthermore, to choose vocational pacifism
would seem logically and morally to require the abandonment
of engaging in relevant dialogue on issues of defense and military strategy with those responsible for the legitimate exercise
of force on behalf of the nation.

The context of the letter is the world of potential conflict
and security needs, where severe differences do in fact exist.
Indeed, conflicts may become more manageable and less
severe precisely because the potential for the use of force is
not abandoned. For example, the existence of the post-war
Western Alliance is surely not unrelated to the political
changes of 1989–1990 in Central and Eastern Europe and to
the dissolution of the Soviet Union itself. The recognition of
such realities seems to be implicit in the bishops' call to
national leaders to put greater emphasis on military restraint
and negotiation. Such a call, however, while praiseworthy,
appears contradictory since it would be unnecessary if violence (force) were in fact to be abandoned, as previously
called for. Restraint and negotiation imply continued reliance
on a credible force structure, not its repudiation.

Conflicting Voices at the 1982 Convention

More substantive and adequate in presenting past teachings of the Christian tradition, the General Convention in 1982
accepted the report of the Joint Commission on Peace entitled
"To Make Peace."[8] The report attempts to root itself in scripture, theology, and the Christian tradition on war and peace.
Based on the classical just war tradition, it argues for the
moral legitimacy of an adequate military defense capability.
While a commitment to absolute pacifism may be attractive, a
majority of the commission considered pacifism to be "impossible." The commission noted, however, that the very factors
that make pacifism impossible make active peacemaking
obligatory.

This perspective reflects the commission's recognition of
the "dual citizenship" of Christians in this world and the legitimate demands of both allegiances. The report then seeks to

help Episcopalians think through and live out their dual obligations as Christian citizens in light of the nuclear dilemma. The effort of the report to maintain the tension represented by the dual citizenship obligations of Christians in this world, rather than to opt for honoring one at the cost of abdicating the other, is in keeping with the Anglican tradition. If nothing else, this emphasis should alert the faithful to any too-easy solution to the nuclear dilemma, whether it be a technically-perfect and impenetrable defensive shield, an overwhelmingly-powerful nuclear superiority, or a morally-pure unilateral disarmament.

More specifically, "To Make Peace" recognizes the dilemma presented to us by the "human need for national security" and, at the same time, the real possibility of nuclear war. It states, "A strategy of nuclear deterrence is at best a necessary evil for a short term." This statement is based on the commission's judgment that nuclear arsenals cannot continue to grow and play a major role in defense postures without eventually being used. The report, therefore, calls for "significant steps toward the control, reduction, and eventual elimination of nuclear weapons." Christians, it claims, can accept nuclear deterrence on moral grounds only if at the same time they understand that its primary purpose is to buy time to work for other, less apocalyptic alternatives. Finally, the report condemns all deterrence strategies that are "based on the intentional and indiscriminate destruction of population centers." The direct and intentional taking of innocent life is judged to be clearly contrary to Christian faith and tradition. While consequences cannot be ignored in relating faith to public policy, they are not the ultimate concern and must always be evaluated morally in conjunction with intentions and the intrinsic nature of specific acts.

While the 1982 General Convention accepted the report of the Joint Commission on Peace, it adopted at the same time three resolutions which seemed either to contradict what was accepted in "To Make Peace," to be counterproductive, or to be unlikely to achieve the ends intended. One resolution endorsed a bilateral nuclear freeze as a first step toward a reduction of nuclear weapons. Specifically, the resolution called for a halt to "the testing, production and further deployment of all nuclear weapons, missiles and delivery systems in a way that can be verified on both sides." The resolution also urged a verifiable across-the-board reduction by fifty percent of the two nuclear arsenals. A second resolution called upon the governments of the United States and the Soviet Union to adopt a policy of "no first use" of nuclear weapons. A third called for a reordering of federal budget priorities, from continuing increases in military spending to human services.[9]

The proposal for a nuclear freeze had several problems. First, there was little likelihood in 1982 that a verifiable bilateral freeze could be implemented, a fact leading some to press the United States for a unilateral freeze. Moreover, a freeze would preclude further weapons modernization, thereby halting development of the more accurate and less destructive tactical weapons which, because they are more credible, are more likely to deter war in the first place. Finally, a freeze would stop further developments on such deterrent systems as nuclear submarines and the B-1 and Stealth bombers, but not on countermeasures to overcome such deterrent systems, such as anti-submarine and anti-aircraft technologies. A freeze could, therefore, weaken deterrence, thereby both increasing instability and making actual use of nuclear weapons more likely as the necessary response to an attack insufficiently deterred.

In calling for a no-first-use pledge, the Convention would have had NATO forego first use of nuclear weapons, even in the face of imminent defeat by the overwhelming conventional force superiority of the Warsaw Pact that existed in the 1980s. A no-first-use pledge would have eroded the deterrent effect of NATO and raised the possibility of a successful Soviet attack in Europe using conventional weapons. Such a pledge would thus have made war more, rather than less, likely. A more viable option, both morally and militarily, might have been a "no strategic first-use" pledge. This would have maintained the deterrent value of the threat of possible first use of tactical nuclear weapons against a large conventional attack, while giving added assurance against a NATO strategic first strike. Finally, any responsible effort to secure a no-first-use pledge would have had to address the issue of the imbalance of conventional forces in Europe. In order for a no-first-use pledge to be a morally responsible option, it would have to have been tied either to the upgrading of NATO conventional forces, and the increase in defense expenditures that would entail, or to the reduction of the conventional forces of the Warsaw Pact. It is at least arguable that the disintegration of the Warsaw Pact after 1989 might not have occurred so readily had resolutions such as this been adopted as government policy at the time they were advocated.

The third resolution from the 1982 General Convention, asking for a reordering of budget priorities, can be read to imply that military spending provides no necessary service to human beings. The question of whether spending is too high, or wasted on unnecessary items, is of course always a debatable issue with definite moral implications. It is misleading, however, to imply that military spending per se does not serve at least one of the needs of human communities, namely, the need for adequate security to protect basic values and freedom. It is, of course, necessary—as the resolution can also be read to imply—for military spending to be realistically evaluated in light of the need for *other* necessary human services, given the limited resources available. Such an interpretation is more in keeping with the Anglican tradition. But such evaluation should be done without a bias against military expenditures per se, be based on adequate knowledge, and refrain from a degree of specificity that is inappropriate for those not directly responsible for the necessary concrete decisions.

At the same 1982 Convention at which the House of Bishops accepted the report of the Joint Commission on Peace, "To Make Peace," the bishops also issued a pastoral letter, "Identity, Pilgrimage and Peace,"[10] which was significantly at odds with some of the work of the Joint Commission. Nearly half of the letter was devoted to the nuclear arms race. The bishops properly recognized that Christians may disagree on the means for achieving peace and that devoted Christians serve in the armed forces. In addition, they raised several issues of concern about the United States' nuclear weapons policy, calling upon the United States to "take the bold initiative in nuclear disarmament," especially since it was the first nation to possess such weapons and the only nation to have used them in war.

In the statement of their concerns, the bishops claimed that the United States' policy of nuclear deterrence included the intention to use nuclear weapons in a massive first strike against whole cities if that would serve the national interest in warfare. They denounced such an intention as evil, as contrary both to the nation's commitment to justice and to the principle of noncombatant immunity. They also declared immoral and unjust "the undiminished production and deployment of nuclear weapons" which, "even if never used," consume enormous economic, technical and natural resources. "The squandering of such resources," the bishops declared, "constitutes an act of aggression against the thirty children who die every sixty seconds of starvation in the world" and manifests "a callous act of indifference" toward the hungry. Finally, the 1982 letter claimed the "American fever to match the Soviet Union weapon for weapon" damages the personality structure of the young and impairs both their ability to form stable values and their sense of purpose. A "belligerent nuclear arms policy" defeats the free nations from within, and, it is implied, causes "the decadence that marks our culture."

The bishops' pastoral, "Identity, Pilgrimage and Peace," is flawed both by some factual errors and by questionable analysis in its expression of its stated concerns. The bishops are in error, for example, in claiming that should deterrence fail, the United States' policy calls for a massive first-strike, counter-city attack. The United States' policy for more than three decades is more properly described as a strategy of flexible response. This is not to claim that no cities are targeted, though precise targets are classified and would be determined in part by the nature of an adversary's attack. Moreover, the United States does not have a first-strike capability, that is to say, the capability of preemptively and systematically destroying all enemy targets capable of launching missiles in retaliation. The bishops were clearly correct to denounce any intentional counter-city strategy, as did the Joint Commission. But the possibility of targeting cities would be, ironically, increased to the extent that arguments of some church groups opposing *all* nuclear weapons modernization came to be accepted. Such arguments, which would halt improvements in the effectiveness of weapons against precise military targets (counterforce targeting), are based on the belief that such improvements might be provocative or make war more likely. The result, however, would quite likely be to increase reliance on the morally unacceptable threat to attack large population centers as the most viable alternative nuclear strategy, given the limitations on improving accuracy.

The bishops' second concern, that there is an excessive use of resources devoted to nuclear weaponry, is based on questionable analysis. Nuclear weapons are, in fact, less expensive than the conventional forces that would be necessary to provide an alternative and equivalent degree of security and deterrence. Nuclear weapons, however one may judge them on other moral or military grounds, actually conserve resources which can be used for other purposes. That is indeed one of the reasons the United States has given them such an excessively important role in its overall defense strategy in the past several decades. The bishops' related concern for the millions in the world who are hungry arises, as it should, out of a fundamental Christian moral imperative. But the sentiment expressed about military expenditures could be applied to *any* expenditure of *any* funds, public or private, so long as anyone is hungry. The question is really whether *any* military expenditures are required of the nation and, if so, which ones and how much. If certain weapons are in fact needed for defense, as determined by a mix of political, prudential, military, and moral judgments, then using resources for that purpose is not automatically to be labelled "squandering" or "a callous act of indifference" toward those with other needs. The expenditures may be excessive, but that is a different issue.

The bishops' discussion of deterrence policy needs to be questioned further with reference to their statement that "the undiminished production and deployment of nuclear weapons, even if never used," consume enormous economic, technical and natural resources. The phrase, "even if never used," seems to imply that expenditures on weaponry are even more wasteful if the weapons are not actually used. The primary aim of such expenditures on weapons, of course, is to prevent war and thus to make their actual use in war unnecessary. If the weapons are never used, and their failure to be used was precisely because of their existence, the cost of the weapons was probably money well spent. That is precisely what a deterrent is supposed to do and is in fact what it has done since World War II. The events of 1989–1990 in Central and Eastern Europe were certainly not unrelated to that fact.

Finally, the 1982 letter expressed concern about the effect of nuclear weapons on personality structures and traits, as well as on the quality of the American culture. It is doubtless true that the international tensions involved in what President Kennedy called our "long twilight struggle" have had some negative impact on people and culture. On the other hand, it is unlikely that the *failure* of the nation to provide for its own and its allies' defense would have quenched the sense of fear, menace, and helplessness identified in the studies to which the bishops referred in expressing their concerns. Furthermore, it is doubtful that the "decadence that marks our culture" is any more attributable to arms policy than it is to other contemporary cultural phenomena, for example, the emphasis on rights over responsibilities or self-actualization over societal obligation.

Questions About Specific Policy Recommendations

In addition to the factual and analytical issues raised above, questions can be raised also about some of the judgments made by the House of Bishops and the General Convention on specific policies. For example, at the 1983 House of Bishops meeting the bishops expressed opposition to the then-imminent installation of Pershing II and Cruise intermediate-range nuclear missiles, the so-called Euromissiles, in Western Europe.[11] Such installation, they declared, would make "the danger of an atomic war by accident, miscalculation or intent greater than ever." It might also set off, they claimed, a further escalation in the arms race. The bishops, therefore, called upon the United States "to delay or to abandon altogether any plans to install these weapons and to intensify negotiations leading to mutually verifiable reduction of nuclear arms."

In view of the Intermediate Nuclear Force (INF) agreement between the United States and the Soviet Union, signed in Washington in December 1987, both the goal and argument of the bishops' resolution were in error. Had the recommended policy—which was also widely supported by various antinuclear groups—become governmental policy, there would likely have been no INF agreement. The several hundred Soviet SS-20 medium-range missiles installed in Eastern Europe in the 1970s, whose removal was the primary purpose of the Euromissiles, would in all probability have remained in place. That could have permanently altered the balance of power in Europe and weakened that military and political link between the United States and its European allies which is the basis of the NATO alliance. Contrary to the expressed fear that the INF deployment would increase the danger of war or cause an escalation in the arms race, it in fact decreased the danger of war and made possible the first arms control agreement in history that actually mandated the destruction of a whole class of nuclear weapons. It thereby allowed for the "mutually verifiable reduction in nuclear arms" which the bishops desired but which would likely have been thwarted if deployment of Euromissiles had been abandoned, as the bishops asked. It also helped to set the stage for the even more dramatic events in Europe two years later, a harbinger of the end of the Cold War and the collapse of the Soviet Union. As *The Economist* said of the Euromissile installation, "it gave peace a chance."

At their 1983 meeting the House of Bishops also asked the Joint Commission on Peace to conduct a study of "the psychology and morality of deterrence" and its particular application to the nuclear arms race. The purpose was to help the Episcopal Church give prudential guidance to its members on the moral questions raised as they seek to exercise the responsibilities of citizenship. The bishops noted their concern that "the strategy of deterrence is the centerpiece of both United States and Soviet policy," but that many questions about the morality of these policies remain unanswered. The requested study was presented to the bishops in July 1984. The study was an eighteen-page document that outlined a series of deterrent strategies, along with some of the political, military, moral, and psychological rationale for and against each strategic option. Its intention was to initiate rather than foreclose discussion, so it did not recommend one preferred position. The study was printed in the 1985 commission reports to the 68th General Convention.[12] The Convention referred it to the church for critical study and reflection, along with statements on deterrence from the World Council of Churches, the Episcopal Diocese of Washington, and the Roman Catholic bishops. As is most often the case, no attempt has been made to determine if these documents were used. It appears, though, that they were not used to any significant degree.

In the General Convention in 1985 three resolutions were passed which reflect something of the stance of the pastoral letters from the House of Bishops. First, the Convention expressed firm opposition to the administration's Strategic Defense Initiative (SDI), the space-based defense plan sometimes referred to as "Star Wars." Second, the Convention again asked Episcopalians to "support and work for a verifiable bilateral nuclear freeze and the continuation of the SALT II accord" and also to "influence government leaders and the producers of military technology and hardware to examine their moral and social responsibility."[13] In a third resolution the Convention again expressed concern about the trend in federal budgeting "away from meeting basic human needs both at home and abroad in preference to increasing the defense establishment."[14]

Both the technical and moral debates about SDI were then and still are important and complex, and much is yet unknown about it. Some of its proponents and opponents made rather premature judgments about SDI, uncritically embracing or rejecting it, without waiting for the facts necessary before full evaluative analysis could be responsibly made about its technical feasibility, strategic usefulness, and moral permissibility. There are major questions about SDI: Will it work? Will it replace deterrence as advertised or only supplement it? Will it escalate the arms race? Is it too costly? Can it be easily and cheaply neutralized? While significant but decreasing funds are still being allocated for SDI research and development, it seems increasingly unlikely that these questions can be answered in ways that would ever make such a "missile defense shield" viable. Nevertheless, in 1985 it was a bit premature, if not presumptuous, for a large body of non-experts to declare itself not only opposed to this complex defense system, about which even the experts needed more information, but also opposed even to studying its feasibility.

The concept of SDI, however unlikely it is that it will ever be a reality, was essentially to deploy a defensive shield rather than an offensive threat, to provide defense by denial rather than defense by retaliation. This goal, however unrealistic or utopian, in effect put the Reagan administration in the "peace movement," at least in the sense that both declared a deterrence policy of mutually assured destruction (MAD) to be immoral and claimed to be seeking a morally preferable alternative. It is noteworthy that the General Convention did not attempt to engage the issue at the moral level—the level that would appear to be the most appropriate for it—especially in light of the relationship of the SDI debate to the issue of the morality of deterrence which the previous Convention and the subsequent work of the Joint Commission on Peace had highlighted.

While the nuclear freeze policy has already been discussed, that portion of the second resolution calling for Episcopalians to exhort government leaders and those who produce military technology to "examine their moral and social responsibility" raises another issue: the intent of the resolution with regard to the question of vocation. Why should these categories of persons be singled out since such examination is presumably expected of all Christians? Does the resolution intend to imply that there is something morally questionable about these vocations per se—a view held by some sectarian Christian communities—or simply to remind such persons that their decisions and actions can have more profound implications for others than is perhaps true of some other vocations? This resolution is unfortunately of little use. There is no indication of what the moral and social responsibility of those involved in government and defense might be, no recognition that one's vocational role carries with it its own moral and social responsibilities that may be in tension with other responsibilities, and no direction for those Episcopalians called upon to do the influencing.

Further Judgments

At the House of Bishops meeting in 1987, the bishops adopted a resolution entitled "The Arms Race, Disarmament and Nuclear Deterrence."[15] The resolution, according to the Religious News Service, did three things: (1) commended the United States and the Soviet Union for their progress toward reducing the numbers of intermediate nuclear forces (INF); (2) urged the United States to work toward a reduction in strategic nuclear weapons; and (3) expressed hope that the INF reductions were "only the first step toward the ultimate and early abandonment of a strategy based on nuclear deterrence or mutually assured destruction." Again, judgments were made without due regard for their moral and political implications and without recognition of the irony of the commendation of the INF treaty in light of the bishops' earlier opposition to the actions that in all likelihood made the treaty possible.

With regard to the third resolution, it is not clear whether the bishops intended to *equate* "a strategy based on nuclear deterrence" with "mutually assured destruction" and to reject that double-named strategy, or to recognize the difference and reject them both. If the former was intended, the bishops should have been made aware that MAD is not the only form of deterrence and that is it not morally necessary to oppose *all* strategies of deterrence because this *one* is morally unacceptable. If the latter was intended, the bishops would have needed to consider what they would propose to put in the place of deterrence. Deterrence has its risks, but the failure to deter also has risks. Taking one set of risks is as morally problematic as taking the other, and in order to judge the morality of deterrence it is always necessary to judge the morality of the alternatives.

For example, to abandon as morally unacceptable *all* strategies of nuclear deterrence in *all* forms would raise several morally relevant issues. In 1987, when no one foresaw the rapid movement toward democracy and free markets that began in 1989 in Soviet bloc nations, such abandonment would have moved the superpower relationship into an unstable and dangerous situation of imbalance and would doubtless have made the events of 1989 less likely. The possibility of nuclear blackmail would have been a real one. Without fear of nuclear retaliation, the long-term Soviet desire to sever Western Europe politically and militarily from the United States might have been realized. To abandon deterrence entirely would even now create certain risks and would do nothing in itself to eliminate the risk of nuclear war. It would only place the decision about war wholly in the hands of those possessing nuclear weapons. It is a historical fact, of course, that the only time nuclear weapons were used was at a time when one side possessed such weapons and the other did not.

In advocating strategic weapons reductions, it is not clear what the bishops understood to be the function of the remainder of the United States' strategic nuclear arsenal. Was the intention of the bishops to maintain an "objective" or "existential" deterrent along the lines advocated by the Roman Catholic bishops, deterring the use of nuclear weapons simply by possessing such weapons without a declared or real intention to use them? Or was it the bishops' intention that all nuclear weapons be given up, multilaterally if possible and unilaterally if necessary? To call for the "early abandonment of a strategy based on nuclear deterrence" requires addressing such questions. If, on the other hand, a strategy of nuclear deterrence of some kind is to be maintained for the foreseeable future, then the question becomes, "What kind of deterrence strategy, if any, can be accepted and defended on moral grounds? Consistently, the bishops have failed to address such questions.

In 1988, issues concerning war, peace, and deterrence did not have as prominent a place in the deliberations of this General Convention as in other Conventions. Reaffirming the sentiment of some past resolutions, one resolution did again urge the United States and the Soviet Union to continue working for reductions in nuclear weapons and to use the funds saved from current and future disarmament agreements to minister to social and human needs. While such reductions are generally desirable, there was again no recognition that numbers of weapons are not as important as the stability allowed and encouraged by the weapons continuing to exist. A second resolution described conscientious objection as a faithful Christian response to a nation's participation in or preparation for war. And a third resolution commended to parishes and dioceses for study and reflection the 1986 statement of the United Methodist bishops entitled "In Defense of Creation: The Nuclear Crisis and a Just Peace."[16]

The resolution reaffirming conscientious objection was in fact the result of the Episcopal Peace Fellowship's effort to pass a different resolution which declared that the normative response of a member of the Episcopal Church was "nonviolent refusal to participate in or prepare for war."[17] The General Convention rejected this pacifist proposal, which would have been a major alteration in the church's historic position, and eventually altered the resolution to reaffirm the church's long-standing position of support for the moral legitimacy of conscientious objection. In engaging the proposal, however, the Convention did not use the opportunity to address either the issue of vocational pacifism or the more complex issue of selective conscientious objection. The latter position seems to be implicit in the Christian just war tradition and therefore a more appropriate and challenging issue, especially since it, unlike vocational pacifism, is not recognized by law.

The resolution commending to the church the United Methodist document also began with an Episcopal Peace Fellowship resolution asking the Convention to adopt as its own the position of the United Methodist bishops who declared, "We conclude that nuclear deterrence is a position which cannot receive the church's blessing."[18] This resolution was defeated, and in its place the Convention merely commended the United Methodist document as a whole for study and reflection. It is, of course, doubtful that many ever thought that a policy of nuclear deterrence should receive the church's blessing in the first place. For a church body to take a position on a morally ambiguous public policy question is not to be equated with blessing that policy. The attempt to equate the two almost appears to be an effort to place those who would defend nuclear deterrence, in whatever form, in the camp of idolators. Indeed, the word idolatry is used more than once in the Methodist document with reference to those who would continue to support a nuclear deterrence policy. Such categorization is hardly an encouragement to engage in the dialogue that the document elsewhere claims to seek. While this is not the place to offer an analysis of the Methodist document, the document has received negative theological critiques from two of the United Methodist Church's own best-known Christian ethicists, the late Paul Ramsey, who was a foremost just war theorist, and Stanley Hauerwas, who is a pacifist.[19]

Recommendations for Developing Moral Teaching

In light of this rather detailed survey, it does not seem unfair to conclude that the position of the Episcopal Church on issues of war, peace, and deterrence is unclear. Indeed, the church's teaching is at times muddled, inconsistent, self-contradictory, and unfocused in its moral appeal. Some of the statements have not been thought through with respect to their implications, both moral and practical, or have not been subjected to rigorous theological, ethical, or political analysis. There is no clearly identifiable theological or ethical tradition, Anglican or otherwise, on which the various positions and policies advocated are based. At the same time, the pronouncements are clearly compassionate, humane, morally earnest, and manifest a deep and genuine concern for peace and justice in the world.

The question for the church is how it might remedy the inadequacies in its statements and teachings while maintaining these positive qualities. What follows, in necessarily short compass, are eight recommendations of ways to begin to answer that question. The preceding analysis has been an exercise in descriptive and critical ethics. The recommendations that follow are offered as a step toward developing a constructive ethic, with the hope that they might contribute to greater clarity and coherence in the church's moral discourse. The first three recommendations are direct responses to what has been said. The other five are related in a more general way to the church's effort to address public policy issues.

1. The church needs to clarify its views on the continuing relevance of the classical just war (or justifiable war) tradition.

The just war tradition has long been the prevailing stance in the Anglican Communion, as well as in the Roman Catholic, Lutheran, and Reformed churches. If the Episcopal Church wishes to reject this 1600-year-old moral tradition, it should say so clearly. The weight of the evidence, however, indicates that it does not. It should, therefore, reaffirm its commitment to, and clarify its understanding of, the just war criteria and their implications both for determining justice in going to war (*jus ad bellum*) and justice in the conduct of war (*jus in bello*). The church should then use the moral framework provided by the classical just war tradition as a base from which to speak with consistency and coherence on contemporary political and military issues.[20]

If the church wishes to engage in the moral debate on political and military issues, and wishes to do so on other than pacifist grounds, there seems to be no morally acceptable alternative to the just war tradition. The fact that it can be, and has been, mis-used is no argument for its abandonment. So long as the world is a place in which defenseless neighbors and fundamental values may be threatened or attacked, moral clarity is necessary for determining if, when, and how the use of force is morally justi-fied and what limitations might be morally required in its exer-cise. The moral choices implied by just war considerations may be unacceptable to those guided only by the vision of a world without violence. But in a world where there are still threats to basic values, the just war tradition is still relevant for Christians seeking to work out the implications of the moral obligations to respond to such threats.

2. The church needs to state more consciously and intention-ally what it means when it speaks of peace.

Sometimes the church uses the term peace in the ultimate sense of shalom. Shalom is the peace that passes understanding, the peace of God who is the author of peace, the peace of a per-fect relationship among human persons, the creation, and God. Such a peace is more than the absence of conflict. It is indeed the eschatological vision of things promised and hoped for, the real-ization of the messianic kingdom at the end of time.

At other times the church uses the word peace in a more lim-ited, political sense, symbolized by the Latin *pax*. This is the peace of the ordered, relatively free political community that makes normal communal living possible. It is peace as the absence of conflict, or at least its minimization and control. Such a state of affairs is not to be denigrated in this world. Peace in this sense has to do with proximate justice, compromise, negotiation, prudence, and considerations of balance of power. The achieve-ment of such a generally acceptable balance between order and liberty in the human community is based upon sometimes fragile mutual agreement and is usually backed up by force.

Too often the church fails to distinguish between these two different meanings of peace. In addition, many who speak for the church tend to use the phrase "peace and justice" almost as if it were one word. When they do this they fail to acknowledge the tension between the two terms. The pursuit of justice may at times require the disruption of an existing state of peace; con-versely, an existing peace may be maintained only by accepting the injustices that may exist within a peaceful community.

The fullness of *shalom* is, finally, a divine gift. It is not an immediate possibility. Yet Christians are called to witness to the Christian vision of peace and to help create the conditions for its appearance to the greatest extent possible. On the other hand, a modest increase in the peaceful nature of a community (*pax*) is at every moment a possibility and is therefore part of the Christian's task. Such modest steps, which can also be negated at any moment, are fragmentary signs and foretastes of the promise of *shalom*. To maintain its credibility in public debate, the church must be careful not to conflate these two understandings of peace.

3. The church needs to relate more explicitly the political and theological aspects of the goal of peace, namely security and reconciliation.

Security refers to the temporal security of a people and a territory. It is a political concept and belongs to the essence of the state. The state is to promote peace but may be obligated to engage in war in order to protect vital security interests and to restore peace through the use of force. Reconciliation, on the other hand, is a theological concept which does not belong to the essence of the state. Indeed, the vulnerability for which security is the intended antidote may be accepted freely for the sake of reconciliation. Christians are called to be agents of reconciliation, to break down barriers, heal wounds, replace enmity and alienation with justice and love, even at the risk of security.

Theologically, the state is intended to be a divine instrument of order in a fallen world. Its purposes include holding the world together by maintaining temporal peace, repelling foes, and shielding the innocent. Providing temporal security, the state can provide time and space for the preaching of the gospel. By participating in this political task the state cooperates in God's work of preservation and thereby may help lay the groundwork for reconciliation. Political security, therefore, has theological implications, even though ultimate security is found in God rather than in any temporal political or military security arrangement.

In turn, reconciliation has political implications. Societies cannot exist by force alone. More power does not necessarily mean more security. In fact, the luxury of security guaranteed by military power is not a possibility in a nuclear age. It is precisely this fact that makes reconciliation an essential component of any prudent security policy. Political prudence now dictates what Christian ethics has always sought, a politics of reconciliation. This requires efforts to overcome hostilities, reconcile interests, and strengthen the elements of community in a national and international society. In short, such a politics of reconciliation is a Christian moral imperative and, at the same time, the highest form of prudential political wisdom in determining a security policy.

4. The church needs to exercise greater care in its use of the word prophetic, especially as applied to itself.

Individuals, and at times institutions, may indeed speak in ways that are prophetic in the biblical sense, seeking in social structures the justice and righteousness that a loving and just God requires. The word prophetic, however, is sometimes used rather too glibly to refer to positions which individuals happen to like, which safely appeal to the proclivities of an audience, or which seem the most radical and therefore supposedly the most authentic. Such statements may in fact be prophetic. But they may also be misuses of the term in order to undergird predetermined ideological views or to give religious respectability to what may in fact be irrational or irresponsible. The prophetic is often proclaimed too easily because the prophet bears no responsibility for the relevant decision or its consequences. For the sake of its credibility—as well as its effectiveness when it does speak a truly prophetic word—the church needs to exercise greater care in issuing what it claims are prophetic proclamations. Prophetic must at least include what it means to the prophets: calling the community back to the values and moral standards in its tradition that it seems to have forgotten.

5. The church needs to reclaim the "church" ecclesiology most associated historically with the Anglican tradition.

With reference to ecclesiology the church needs to do at least two things. It needs to place a renewed emphasis on the church as a worshipping community and to reaffirm the church as church as opposed to sect. First, the church in its essence is a worshipping community. All else stems from that. Worship exists for its own sake and is not to be used for utilitarian or partisan purposes. It is only *because* the church is a worshipping community that it seeks to live out its self-understanding as a reconciling, witnessing, peacemaking, justice-seeking community. That may be done well or poorly, with prophetic vision or simplistic moralism. At times the church will fail. Still, the church is called to be faithful, not necessarily successful, knowing that ultimately history is in God's hands and not ours.

On the other hand, the church as a worshipping community is not true to its call if it does nothing *but* worship. Worship and moral deliberation and action are distinct but interrelated activities. While it is not the reason we worship, nothing can better form the primary moral affections and intentions of Christian people than the regular exposure to, and reiteration of, the liturgical acts and words experienced as part of a worshipping Christian community.

The second ecclesiological theme draws on the classical distinction between church and sect. Each type has its correlative mode of addressing public policy issues. The church-type, to which the Episcopal Church belongs historically, has a broad and inclusive concept of the religious community and assumes some responsibility for the moral ethos of the society, its civic virtues and its public morality. It believes it has some insights into the intention of God the Creator for the whole human community and an obligation to relate those insights in politically relevant ways to the conduct of public affairs. It recognizes the appropriateness of Christians themselves exercising positions of responsibility in and for the structures of society.

In contrast to the church, the sect-type ecclesiology has a more exclusive view of the religious community. It emphasizes Christian discipleship and the distinctive quality of the Christian life as over-against the rest of society. The Christian vocation is exercised more in witnessing to the authenticity of its vision than in being in dialogue with the kingdoms of this world, more in confronting Caesar's household than in participating in the order-maintaining and justice-dispensing tasks of political order. The sect is suspicious of Christian involvement in the functions of the public realm. It focuses more on the holy fellowship than on the ambiguities of the exercise of power in a fallen world.

The church- and sect-type ecclesiologies each have had distinctive ethical implications. Out of the church has come the justifiable war tradition; out of the sect has come the pacifist tradition. Out of the church has come the tradition of the Christian magistrate dealing in the shades of gray of political compromise in order to maintain some semblance of social harmony and community. Out of the sect has come the witness of the outsider to the vision of *shalom*, without which we may not know the difference among the various shades of gray.

While both church and sect traditions have strengths and dangers, historically the Anglican communion has belonged primarily to the church-type tradition. Today it needs to reaffirm that tradition and the culture-forming task which accompanies it. This reaffirmation is needed not only for the church to be true to its heritage. It is also needed because of the rapid rise in recent years of the "naked public square" in our increasingly secular society, the moral rootlessness thereby encouraged, and the disintegrative tendencies of American individualism that would gladly leave the greater society to take care of itself. Whatever the contribution of the sectarian witness, only the church tradition has a theology, a worldview, and a moral tradition adequate to combat effectively the ethical emotivism and the self-destructive tendencies of modern society.

6. The church needs to exercise more carefully its teaching responsibility both to inform conscience and to participate in shaping the terms of public debate; moreover, it needs to be clear which purposes it is pursuing in its teaching at a particular time.

The tasks of formation of conscience and engaging issues in public life are both essential. The formation of conscience apart from addressing public life can lead to political irrelevance. Engaging political issues without attention to what is distinctively Christian can result in the co-optation of moral teaching by the rulers of this world. The Roman Catholic bishops were attempting to fulfill both tasks in their pastoral letters on war and peace and on the economy. They, moreover, made an effort to distinguish between these two tasks. They recognized the legitimate preserving, ordering, and enabling functions of the political and economic realms while offering a clear Christian vision that provided a basis for a relevant and informed moral critique of public policy regarding the use of force and the economic order. The Episcopal Church should exercise its teaching functions with no less precision and clarity.

7. The church needs to recognize and honor more explicitly the classical Reformation doctrine of vocation.

While the Roman Catholic Church has picked up the theme of vocation in significant ways under the rubric of "the apostolate of the laity," the Episcopal Church's emphasis in recent years on lay ministry seems to have missed a major part of the meaning of vocation by stressing what lay people do within the institutional church. What is needed is the broader understanding that the church is the people of God, both gathered in community and scattered in the world. It is in the latter form that Christians, through their "secular" vocations, exercise most directly their vocation and ministry to serve God and neighbor. It is through the responsible exercise of the duties and responsibilities of their daily work that Christians maintain the fabric of God's world. Such tasks have nothing to do with the institutional church in a narrow or official sense.

This important Reformation emphasis on vocation gave the ordinary run of human work the Christian dignity that had traditionally belonged only to the clergy. It taught that the true test of a Christian vocation was not its spirituality but the quality of its service to the neighbor and to the common good. Such teaching invigorates the laity in the performance of their work by enabling them to see their daily work of production and distribution, farming and teaching, homemaking and soldiering, as high callings.

If the laity, however, properly exercising their Christian calling in their daily work, have developed an expertise in their vocations that surpasses that of the representatives of the institutional church, the question must be asked, "What is it appropriate for the institutional church to say to the scattered church about its worldly tasks?" When does the institutional church inappropriately impinge on the work of the laity, especially those with political, economic, or military responsibilities? At what point does appropriate moral exhortation and conscience formation become inappropriate involvement in technical issues? These are, of course, not new questions. They are, though, questions that the church must constantly address as it goes about its task of relating its faith to moral issues of the day.

Too often, ecclesiastical bodies overstep the boundary between what the late Paul Ramsey described as giving *direction* to public policy and issuing *directives* for legislative and administrative action. There is a fine line between them that is not always easy to identify. Sometimes the church probably should issue directives regarding policy decisions. The more specific such teachings become, however, the less can be the degree of theological and ethical certitude and the greater the probability of legitimate disagreement between the institutional church and thoughtful Christians in their various vocations.

8. Finally, the church needs to reaffirm its traditional theological understanding of the role of the political order in fostering, preserving, and maintaining a just and humane human community.

The church must recognize the *relative* autonomy of the political realm. This means that the church must promote a concern for civic virtue while avoiding both co-optation by the powers of the world and a narrow compartmentalization of religion and politics. It also means that the church must avoid a too-easy resort to the language of moral equivalance in politics as a substitute for making moral choices among lesser evils and relative goods. An adequate understanding of the relation between faith and politics has been variously conceptualized in different traditions, for example, by such terms as two cities, two swords, two kingdoms, two governments, and two ways in which God governs the world. Whatever the terminology for expressing this twofoldness, some such concept seems necessary to avoid either absolutizing the political task or denying to it any theological significance at all. Neither messianic politics nor political indifference can march properly under the banner of Christianity. Religious obligations and political obligations are never to be equated, yet each has important implications for the other.

The fundamental mission of the church is to proclaim the gospel of Jesus Christ, not to give unquestioning moral legitimacy to any political status quo or to any alternative to the status quo. The dead are not raised by politics, and politics is not the realm of redemption. Only the gospel can liberate us, and that relativizes all our other projects in this world, including genuinely important and morally relevant political projects. If we are grounded in the gospel, we are grounded in something beyond politics. We are then more likely to be effective in the political order and in its task of building and maintaining a just and humane community. Rooted in that which is transcendent, we are then free to deal soberly and prudently with political reality, instead of identifying a particular political agenda with the church and, by implication, excluding those who may dissent.

Endnotes

1. *Cross Before Flag: Episcopal Statements on War and Peace* (Washington, D.C.: Episcopal Peace Fellowship, Revised Edition, 1986.)

2. "Identity, Pilgrimage and Peace," *Journal of the General Convention,* 1982, p. A-4.

3. *Journal of the General Convention,* 1964, p. 980. See also *Cross Before Flag,* p. 19.

4. For the full text of the 1962 pastoral letter, see *Journal of the General Convention,* 1964, pp. 980–984. This and some other key segments of the letter are omitted from the *Cross Before Flag* excerpts.

5. A discussion of the criteria of the 1600-year-old just (or justifiable) war tradition and their interpretation is beyond the scope of this paper. The criteria are listed in the appendix of the first report of the Joint Commission on Peace (see endnote #8) and in the National Conference of Catholic Bishops' pastoral letter, *The Challenging of Peace* (Washington: U.S. Catholic Conference, 3

May 1983), paragraphs 80–110. For more thorough treatment see Paul Ramsey, *War and the Christian Conscience* (Durham: Duke University Press, 1961); James Turner Johnson, *Just War Tradition and the Restraint of War* (Princeton: Princeton University Press, 1981) and *Can Modern War Be Just?* (New Haven, Yale University Press, 1984).

6. *Journal of the General Convention,* 1979, pp. C-106–107. See also *Cross Before Flag,* p. 26.

7. *Journal of the General Convention,* 1982, p. B-213. See also *Cross Before Flag,* p. 28.

8. *To Make Peace: The Report of the Joint Commission on Peace* (Cincinnati: Forward Movement Publications, 1982).

9. *Journal of the General Convention,* 1982, pp. C-125, C-127, C-151. See also *Episcopal Peace Fellowship Newsletter* (Fall 1982), pp. 2–3.

10. *Journal of the General Convention,* 1982, pp. A-2 through A-5.

11. *Journal of the General Convention,* 1985, pp. 306-307. See also *Diocesan Press Service* (12 October 1983), pp. 1–10, 25.

12. *The Blue Book,* 1985, pp. 248–257.

13. *Journal of the General Convention,* 1985, pp. 177–179. See also *Cross Before Flag,* p. 35.

14. Ibid., p. 205.

15. *Journal of the General Convention,* 1988, p. 425.

16. Ibid., pp. 275, 291, 292. See also *The Episcopalian,* Vol. 153 (August 1988) 8:pp. 31–32.

17. Ibid., p. 581. See also *Episcopal Peace Fellowship Newsletter* (Pentecost 1988), p. 5.

18. Ibid., pp. 623–624. See also *Episcopal Peace Fellowship Newsletter* (Pentecost 1988), p. 5, and a letter from the Rev. Nathaniel Pierce to members of the Standing Commission on Peace, 28 August 1988.

19. Paul Ramsey, *Speak Up for Just War or Pacifism* (University Park: Pennsylvania State University Press, 1988).

20. For a recent illustration of the need for such consistency and coherence, see Allan M. Parrent, "The War in the Persian Gulf and the Episcopal Church," *Sewanee Theological Review,* Vol. 35 (Christmas 1991) 1:pp. 13–38. This is a detailed account of how the Episcopal Church responded at the official level to the events leading up to the Gulf War and to U.S. participation in it.

6

The Dispersal of Moral Authority

Ellen K. Wondra

The introductory essay and case studies in this volume discuss in detail the Episcopal Church's public statements on a variety of moral and social issues. These statements address matters of broad public concern which are also matters of public policy. The statements are also intended to form the moral life of the Episcopal Church. But, as the essays argue, however good the statements may be—however humane, comprehensive, and reasoned—far too frequently their general value is diminished by certain flaws.

Timothy Sedgwick argues that many public statements are episodic, hasty, and shallow, more in the nature of "moral declaration" than "broadly informed, reasoned arguments." Harmon Smith says they are "rather more reflexive than reflective." Allan Parrent finds them often self-contradictory, inconsistent, muddled, and chaotic. David Scott judges them to be marred by problems of logic, by avoidance of fundamental issues, and by failure even to identify moral standards. David Smith and Judith Granbois note that the statements ignore pertinent research and opinion available from other, often more expert bodies and from our ecumenical dialogue partners. Allan Parrent sums up the situation by indicating that there is "no clearly identifiable theological or ethical tradition, Anglican or otherwise, on which the various positions and policies advocated are based." Nevertheless,

> At the same time, the pronouncements are clearly compassionate, humane, morally earnest, and manifest a deep and genuine concern for peace and justice in the world. The question for the church is how it might remedy the inadequacies in its statements and teachings while maintaining these positive qualities.[1]

In sum, the Episcopal Church's moral statements often fail to

be persuasive, and they fail to generate agreement or adherence within the church, let alone outside it. What is at stake
here, this volume suggests, is the church's authority in the
lives of its own members *and* the church's credibility in the
larger society which it has some desire to shape if not lead. In
each arena, church and public forum, the Episcopal Church
has not adequately indicated why people should agree with its
statements; nor, the case studies suggest, has it been persuasive in indicating why people inside and outside the church
should listen at all.

The essays in this volume direct our attention not only to
the content of the church's ethical understanding, but also to
its larger self-understanding of itself as a religious body. That
is, they are questions not only in ethics but also in ecclesiology. Further, they direct our attention to the relation between
the church and the world, and so, finally, to the Episcopal
Church's understanding of the human condition and human
relatedness to God. On the basis of how one views these matters, various considered positions on the issues discussed here
may emerge, and the essays here sketch out some possibilities.
It is the purpose of this chapter not to agree or disagree with
the conclusions which the case studies reach on issues, but
rather to focus on the ecclesiological presuppositions which
underlie our discussions and to evaluate some of the proposals made by the other essayists. I will, therefore, touch on theological views of the human, the divine, and their relation, but
I will do this by focusing on the relation of moral authority to
ecclesiology.

For example, in his discussion of the use of military force
in our nuclear age, Allan Parrent considers the ecclesiological
and ethical reasons why this issue is a perennial one. Parrent
argues that there is an inescapable twofoldness in any adequate understanding of the relation between faith and politics
which ought constantly to keep the Episcopal Church in tension between co-optation by the status quo, on the one hand,
and isolationist withdrawal from the public arena, on the
other hand.[2] This analysis is undergirded by Parrent's view of
the Episcopal Church as a church rather than a sect.
Sociologically speaking, churches live their corporate lives in
both sacred and secular realms, differentiating between political realities and ultimate redemption. At the same time, they
seek to modify political realities so that they approximate
within the limitations of history a community which can be

realized fully only beyond history. This churchly view stands in contrast to a more sectarian one—not represented anywhere in this volume—which would take a stance "over against" the morality of "the world" to which the church is thus related as critic rather than as former or transformer.

Churches, Parrent urges, must distinguish *shalom*, or future eschatological and God-given peace, from the realizable *pax*, or civil orderliness which can and must be achieved in history. It is, therefore, no surprise that Parrent also wishes the Episcopal Church's statements to maintain a level of abstraction which will minimize the probability of "legitimate disagreement between the institutional church and thoughtful Christians in their various vocations."[3] Statements that take a specific, prophetic advocacy position either for or against the use of particular kinds of force in concrete situations may appear to foster *shalom*, Parrent thinks; they may in fact, however, more significantly limit the possibilities of *pax*.

One may agree or disagree with this position and with the particular definitions that support it.[4] My point here is simply that Parrent's conclusions about the use of force are consistent with the ecclesiological and theological foundations on which his work is based. In this sense, Parrent's essay provides a helpful example of how moral teachings can be made: the bases of his argument are apparent, and his reasoning follows those bases. He presents reasoned arguments for his conclusions. This allows his readers to determine their consent to or dissent from his position on the basis of adequate evidence and the examination of how persuasive that evidence is in light of their own reason, conscience, and the concrete shape of their lives as Christians.

Timothy Sedgwick's essay on Episcopal Church statements on the economic order addresses the relation of church and society from a different angle, by looking at the presuppositions about the good which are embedded in these statements. Sedgwick discloses three basic convictions that underlie most of the Episcopal Church's statements on the economic order: the absolute value of the individual, the communal character of human life, and freedom as essential to being human.[5] These convictions lead him to conclude that the Episcopal Church is assuming a particular view of human destiny as fulfillment. This view, moreover, can be examined in light of the church's theological understanding of the nature of humanity itself and how humankind is related to

God. Sedgwick argues that the assumption of fulfillment as synonymous with God-intended destiny contributes to a troubling disparity between the incisive analysis recently developed by the Urban Bishops' Coalition and their idealistic recommendations. This disparity leads to moral confusion and to programmatic action which is both ineffective and lacking in credibility.

Consistent with his own analysis, Sedgwick recommends a shift in theological, ethical, and ecclesiological foundations away from views based on purposes to be fulfilled and toward a witness to the experience of grace such that church and world are related sacramentally. That is, the church's purpose is to form persons so that they bear witness to the grace that they encounter, not only in the life of the church but in their encounters with strangers. Concretely, the poor are those through whom God is present and is presently effecting conversion. As Sedgwick presents it, such a view entails not the cessation of transformative involvement between church and society, but its reorientation. Although Sedgwick does not in the limited space of his essay develop this reorientation in detail, presumably it entails concerted work toward redistributing power and resources in order to enable rather than curtail the graciousness of human existence for all.

Again, Sedgwick's shift from an idealistic ethics to one of witness is a helpful example of how moral arguments can be made effectively. His essay enables us to see how fundamental assumptions are expressed in practical statements, and how the disparity between assumptions and programs serves to hamper or defeat both. Again, we may agree or disagree with his conclusions; but we do so on the basis of evidence which is mustered in a way that allows us to reflect on our own assumptions and envisioned actions.

Sedgwick and Parrent, then, present two different options in ecclesiology. Of equal if not greater significance, however, is their illustration of the fact that reasonable, informed, and faithful persons can begin from base positions which demonstrate considerable commonality, and then go on to argue both critically and cogently to quite different conclusions about the sort of ethical orientations toward which moral teaching may lead.

Our concern in the discussions that are reflected in this volume, then, is primarily with processes of moral formation rather than with criticism of particular actions taken or not taken by the Episcopal Church. And moral formation is accomplished *in part* by moral teaching. (It is also nurtured, we should note, by corporate and individual spirituality, by study and reflection, and by action.) We have focused specifically on moral teachings that have some official and national status: that is, on the statements proposed to or made by bodies such as the General Convention, the House of Bishops, and some of the commissions these bodies appoint. We do not assume, however, that moral teaching takes place *only* at the national level. Indeed, corporate moral teaching takes place from the pulpit, in the liturgy itself, in church education programs, through church publications of many sorts, in counseling sessions, in informal gatherings, and in formal bodies such as committees and commissions at congregational and diocesan levels, as well as at the national level.

Our focus on the national level makes sense for at least two reasons. First, in the Episcopal Church, it is national bodies which receive, gather, and distribute resolutions and other materials produced at diocesan and local levels. Therefore, if there is such a thing as the "mind of the Episcopal Church," it is generally reflected in the statements of the national bodies. In this sense, as David Scott notes, these statements are teaching *by* the Episcopal Church as well as *in* it.[6]

Second, and the basis of the first, the Episcopal Church views itself neither as a sect, nor as an aggregate of free associations. Instead, as some of the essays suggest, we see ourselves more as "the body of Christ, whose members have the mind of Christ and are to mature into the fullness of that mind";[7] or as a church, a community with "a theology, a worldview, and a moral tradition" which gather it for worship and spur it to engage in "the culture-forming task" which accompanies such an identity.[8] Consistent with an ecclesiology which understands the gathered church as the body of Christ, the Episcopal Church's *Book of Common Prayer* indicates that it is bishops who have responsibility for moral teachings. This does not mean that only bishops teach—quite the contrary, as David Smith and Judith Granbois remind us. It does mean that bishops in particular are charged with making sure teaching does take place and for overseeing both its occurrence and its quality. That is, it is bishops who have a particular type of authority in regard to moral teaching.

But what else do we mean in our discussions by the word authority? What types of authority do we have in mind?

Where does authority lie, and where ought it to lie? And what is its source? In his introduction to *Authority in the Anglican Communion*, Stephen Sykes suggests that authority is constituted by theology, structure, and practice, and that all three areas should be examined.[9]

As is widely recognized, in practice Protestantism in the United States is a voluntary society. That is, its existence depends on consent—not assent—of will and mind.[10] Theologically, this is entirely in keeping with the Protestant tradition, which deliberately rejects any attempts to limit authority to a particular ecclesial or social caste. Moral authority, like governing authority, is widely dispersed; the Protestant ordinary magisterium is the church itself.

The reasons for this dispersal of authority have to do primarily with Protestantism's own basic theological affirmations, rather than with external factors such as the secularization of modern and post-modern culture. Stephen Sykes makes this point well in relation to authority issues within Anglicanism:

> The possession by ordinary clergy and by the laity of the gospel in their own tongue, interpreted by, and interpreting the liturgy of the church, is crucial for the Anglican understanding of authority. It means that there *actually is* a widely distributed source of authority and a means of judging, independently if need be, whether the truth of the gospel is being upheld by those with the most obvious access to the decision-making process.[11]

According to Protestant theology, the Holy Spirit is given to all, all have direct access to the norms of the faith, and all are obligated to act on the basis of their own informed consciences, guided also by reason. Sykes goes on to say that

> The same Anglican documents . . . also affirm quite unequivocally that there is a hierarchy of ministerial order charged with exercising discipline in various matters. . . . [This] combination of a theological empowering of the whole people of God with a hierarchical structure in the church creates in Anglicanism a tension.[12]

This tension is evident in the public statements and practices of the Episcopal Church, for the dispersal of the moral authority (and so the teaching office of the church, the ordinary magisterium) is reflected in our polity, which is congre-

gational and presbyterian in structure as much as it is episcopal. This threefold structure provides a system of checks
against the abuse of authority by any single element of the
structure. But it also may produce conflicting statements and
practices. And the structure itself raises perennial questions
about who may credibly, persuasively, or decisively claim
authority even to settle the question of who may speak.

Second, we are a church which prides itself (often if not
always) on its comprehensiveness: that is, on our ability to
encompass many theological, religious, moral, and political
views within one body. We value diversity, yet we seek
through that diversity a unity based on a common identity.
The perennial tensions of unity and diversity raise again and
again the questions of the limits of diversity and of the loca-
tion(s) of the sources of identity.

In other words, the Episcopal Church is in part constituted
theologically and structurally by many of the things which
give rise to the very situation we may on occasion find ourselves bemoaning. Inconsistency and even heterodoxy are
always possible; debate about matters of faith and morals is
embedded into the very structures of Protestant denominations, including our own.[13] It is then no wonder that we speak
and act inconsistently, particularly over a considerable period
of time, as is the case with statements about war and peace, or
about economic justice. The question, then, is not how to
eliminate inconsistency, but rather what kinds of inconsistency, and in what areas, are unacceptable, and why?

Yet it is not just our Protestant identity and polity which
aggravate some of the problems identified in this volume. The
Episcopal Church is also a voluntary society in a pluralistic
culture, and this fact points to a dispersal of authority of
another sort. On the one hand, because of the dispersal of
authority,

> Protestant church teachings carry the weight of their
> arguments and little in addition to that. Thus the argu-
> ments have to be developed in an honest and coherent
> way to be at least considered by, and at best persua-
> sive to, the Christian and secular communities. This
> requires clarification and defense of the principles
> that sustain the teachings to both intended audi-
> ences.[14]

On this the essays in this volume are agreed. And the essays
are agreed that such clarification and defense of principles is

often not forthcoming. In part this is, as David Scott and Harmon Smith suggest, because legislative bodies and processes are not conducive *in their very form* to lengthy, careful, and reasoned argument and the development of consensus.

Yet, on the other hand, we should also note that in a voluntary society moral teachings must stay fairly close to "the prevailing moral opinions of church members," or the response is likely to be either indifference or hostility.[15] At the same time, what draws people to Protestant churches and informs their consent of will and mind is as much social class, education, and ethnicity as it is religious or theological identification.[16] In other words, people join churches—including Episcopal churches—for reasons that have less to do with churchly religion than with daily life and culture.

So how does the church speak authoritatively without unduly alienating members who are members voluntarily? And are there theological and religious reasons we should worry about this? David Scott suggests that there are when he wonders whether theology and ethics can appropriately be done by plebiscite. Other essayists—notably Timothy Sedgwick and Harmon Smith—raise concerns about what they deem the politically motivated composition of those commissions, committees, and delegations that recommend and vote on statements that have the force of moral teaching.

I believe we need an understanding of the nature of authority which is consistent with our identity. And our identity is, I have indicated, both Protestant and plural as well as Catholic and structured. Or, to modify Ernst Troeltsch's classic terms, the Episcopal Church as an American religious body is somewhere between sect and church. It is, properly, a denomination. That is, the Episcopal Church is one among many religious institutions which claims to embody in a particular way truths and traditions held in common with others. A denomination is like a church in that it "has a theology, a worldview, and a moral tradition adequate to" its culture-influencing task.[17] Yet it is also like a sect in that it claims a particular identity which distinguishes it from others and which it is necessarily at some pains to define and at times protect. To use scriptural images, denominational Christianity may be less like a body of Christ and more like the branches of a single vine, branches which are of various size and fruitfulness, and which at times prick each other with their thorns. Minimally, denominations tolerate "diverse claims to truth and legitimacy" made by other denominations in the pluralistic society in which all exist;[18] maximally, they seek communion with these others (as the Episcopal Church has with the Evangelical Lutheran Church of America, for example).

This being the case, I should like to propose a definition of authority developed by John Skinner. He states that authority is

> that kind of structured reality, whether social or personal, which through nurture and cultivation [anchored ultimately in the source of all reality] enables individuals to become truly centered selves or persons, and thus, relatively free beings. . . . Structured reality presupposes both a corporate or social dimension to authority, as well as a personal, individual dimension.[19]

Stephen Sykes makes a similar point when he notes, "The positive nature of the authority which binds the Anglican communion together is . . . moral and spiritual, resting on the truth of the Gospel, and on a charity which is patient and willing to defer to the common mind."[20]

The church, made up of "relatively free human beings," is to be "a transparent medium" for "creativity and redemption."[21] Further, as the 1968 Lambeth Conference pointed out, authority must "refuse to insulate itself against the testing of history and the free action of reason,"[22] even— and perhaps especially—when such testing strikes at long-cherished and deeply-held presuppositions and convictions. The church must also form, protect, and nurture the informed consciences of its members, seeking to generate a *consensus fidelium* rather than either assuming or dictating it.

Now, if this is something like the way the Episcopal Church understands authority (and in practice I think it is), then our moral teachings are authoritative only to the extent that they both "rest on the truth of the Gospel" and "nurture and cultivate relatively free human beings who then may encounter a benevolent transcendence through the images and symbols which make up the nurturing matrix."[23] In other words, our moral teachings are authoritative to the extent that they make creative use of the harmonies, tensions, and even conflicts among such diverse sources as scripture, tradition, reason, and experience (the latter two understood in their broadest senses).

What kind of discourse conveys this kind of authority? Certainly, it must be one which uses clear and persuasive arguments. But further, it must be a mode of discourse which involves mutual probing, each participant with his [or her] special skills, his [or her] gifts of wisdom, his [or her] technical knowledge, his [or her] powers of persuasion, enlightening the process toward consensus about what deeds and words are worthy of the gospel, what activities are consonant with the faith, what performances are consistent with and expressive of the beliefs of the church.[24]

In other words, we need to engage in discourse which is dialogical with an intention of identifying, generating, and fostering consensus among the faithful.

Dialogue, I believe, has better possibilities for fostering consensus than proclamations or pronouncements which carry with them the expectation of obedience and loyalty, *even if* those proclamations and pronouncements are made on the basis of clear and sound argument. This is so for a number of reasons.

First, we *are* a diverse community. This is the reality of our situation in a church which is at one and the same time Protestant and Catholic and which gathers in a pluralistic society. And we are diverse not only at the level of which form of liturgy we prefer or of our positions on pressing social issues. As a recent Gallup poll indicates, we are also diverse in our core beliefs about the incarnation, the Trinity, the authority of scripture, and the relation between God's will and individual human will, as well as about abortion, homosexuality, and matters of justice.[25] As Harmon Smith and others in this volume argue, obtaining agreement among such a varied group can happen only with the emergence of common, or shared, beliefs which are connected to a shared life. But it is imperative to note that shared beliefs and a shared life do not *necessarily* require uniform moral dispositions or practices. They do require ongoing critical and generous dialogue, tolerance for diversity and ambiguity, and the widest ranging participation that can be imagined.

Indeed, when our shared life is itself as diverse as it is—when the church attracts members at least as much because of its location and social composition as it does its religious beliefs and practices—we need actually to engage in discourse which recognizes that to some extent truth (and so the good) is intersubjective, that truth is discovered or disclosed by mutual questioning and exploration, and that *any* claim to truth must be subjected to further critical exploration.[26]

Where does such discourse properly take place? We are a community with diverse structures and with widely varying participation in those structures. General Convention, the House of Bishops; and the standing commissions of the church are not the only place where authoritative moral discourse takes place, as David Scott has helpfully noted. Consensus, by definition, is not consensus unless and until all participate. So I would agree here with Timothy Sedgwick's and others' insistence that the Episcopal Church commit more of its resources (material and spiritual) to teaching and less to pronouncing. I would also agree with Allan Parrent's interest in pedagogy as connected to prophecy and moral formation. Indeed, I would reiterate one of Timothy Sedgwick's points: teaching itself can help to "constitute a ground of common convictions and understandings that will not narrowly define Christian faith in terms of particular concerns and convictions."[27] Sedgwick further argues that teaching alone is not sufficient: discipline is needed. But I would suggest that something else is needed as well.

I wish to go further than my colleagues in insisting that we cannot reach a consensus that *is* a true consensus until we address the conditions under which speech takes place in our church and in the society in which the church is set. And here I am referring directly to the issue of participation in the councils of the church as a problem of distribution of power and resources.[28] Who may speak in this church and expect to be heard? Who, even now, is being silenced or ignored?

Answering these questions requires looking not only at the membership of our committees and commissions, our House of Deputies and our House of Bishops, although it does certainly require this. It also entails looking critically at our customary modes of discourse, the grounds of our notions of who is qualified to speak, the issues we choose to address, and the relation of these things to the structures and social composition of our church at every level and function, both as they have been, as they are at the moment, and as we wish them to become. (I think it is significant, for example, that the essays in this volume do not include discussion of the relation of race and gender among the areas of concern they address.) And we need to look, as always, at the theological, ethical, and other presuppositions and claims that are related to our analysis.

We cannot achieve consensus unless and until we give voice to the voiceless among us. In recent discussions of authority and ecclesial decision-making, we have taken our lead from the ordinal, and perhaps particularly from the rite of the Ordination of a Bishop. The emphasis has seemed to fall on the role of the bishop to "guard the faith, unity, and discipline of the Church." Yet it must fall also on the call to "be merciful to all, show compassion to the poor and strangers, and defend those who have no helper."[29] This also is part of moral formation.

Despite the challenges, difficulties, and anxieties associated with broadening representation and modes of discourse in the many councils of the church, and in our understanding of the possibilities of where such counsel is taken, this process must continue, or the possibility of consensus will be lost under an appearance of agreement which is obtained at the cost of the discouragement and departure of some of the faithful and conscientious. Without attention to this area, our pleas for unity hold little promise.[30]

This is not only a concern for the structures and the personnel practices of the Episcopal Church. It is also a theological and ethical concern which pushes the church to examine its presuppositions about moral, ecclesial, and social responsibility. As Sharon D. Welch has recently argued, commonly held notions of responsibility assume that agency is synonymous with observable effectiveness: "what counts as 'responsible action' . . . assumes[s] that to be responsible means that one can ensure that the aim of one's action will be carried out."[31] Yet in situations where authority and power are dispersed, no individual agent can rest on such an assurance. Instead, Welch argues, responsible action entails "not the certain achievement of desired ends but the creation of a matrix in which further actions are possible, the creation of the conditions of possibility for desired changes" in the present and the future. Such action "is sustained and enabled by participation in an extensive community."[32] Responsible action, that is, emerges in dialogue which is not an end in itself but which intends an enlargement of moral vision and "more adequate understandings of what is just and how particular forms of justice may be achieved."[33]

Dialogue has sound theological reasons to commend it as well. If (as our authors assume) all persons do have a common foundation for our lives, if (as our own Prayer Book assures us) Jesus died not for our sins only but for the sins of the whole world; if (as Protestant Christianity believes) the Spirit is given to the whole body of Christ; if (again, as the Prayer Book insists) the church is a witness in the world—if all these things are the case, then our quests for truth, meaning, and guidance ought to reflect that common foundation, and we ought to enlarge our search and our vision as widely as ever we can. Dialogical moral discourse presumes that "God is present, and is seeking to speak [God's] word in the life of the church. Although one cannot claim full confidence that the moral consensus of the church is the voice of God, nevertheless [God's] Spirit is present in human deliberation and action." And humans are nurtured by our participation in the life of God.[34]

Our task, then, would seem to be discovering ways in which we can nurture consensus. How might this be done? The essays in this volume contain many suggestions. David Scott, Timothy Sedgwick, and Allan Parrent urge adoption of the best of the model followed by the American Roman Catholic bishops in their recent pastorals. These pastorals, while issued by the bishops, were crafted collegially by working groups made up of bishops, scholars, priests, and lay people with expertise and interest in the topics. This work also involved dialogue with those outside the church knowledgeable in the matters discussed.

But before the Episcopal Church rushes to adopt this model, we would do well to note which pastorals are held up in these essays, and which are not. Notably not mentioned in this volume are statements whose crafting was not broadly participatory—the draft pastoral on the role of women, for example. These may serve the Episcopal Church as negative examples of the exercise of both ordinary and extraordinary magisterium.

David Smith and Judith Granbois have made a number of suggestions which I find more helpful, and more modest, because more consistent with the ecclesiology I have sketched in this essay. Smith and Granbois suggest that we ought to make better use of the experts among us in the areas of their expertise. They also urge that we focus less on "statements at the national or judicatory level" and more on "the more fundamental task of nourishing discussion and exploration within congregations of inquiring Christian persons."[35] They further propose that the dispersal of moral authority be formally recognized through a deliberate revision of our study and pronouncement processes such that study commissions be authorized by the church, but produce statements which bear the authority not of the church as a body, but of their authors.

This shift in practice and structure would be "visibly willing to proceed in a genuinely humble spirit of inquiry."[36] Such a move would re-establish the difference between the ordinary magisterium and the extraordinary magisterium; it would recognize at the level of institutional practice what is already the case at the level of daily denominational life. The exercise of extraordinary magisterial powers would be reserved as a last resort, to settle controversies which have proven themselves to be resistant to the discipline of prolonged critical and generous dialogue. (What constitutes proof would, I suggest, most appropriately emerge from the process of dialogue itself.) Smith and Granbois conclude,

> we should stress a kind of common law mentality in which we eschew grand statements of principle, trusting rather that moral truth will emerge in educated grapplings with problems by Christians. Consensus is not to be manufactured; it happens, and the process will not be rushed or engineered.[37]

Nor, I would observe, will it finally be curtailed; but it may be moved outside the Episcopal Church.

The kind of change that Smith and Granbois propose will mean, I suspect, that General Convention will have to refuse to make apparently authoritative statements until such discussion and exploration can take place and be studied at congregational and diocesan levels. Further, since, as David Scott and Harmon Smith point out, the General Convention resolution process and genre is not in any case conducive to moral argument, such restraint may also serve the end of clarifying the nature of moral formation.

Such a change will also mean that the Episcopal Church will have to put more energy and resources into pedagogy which is directed at stimulating dialogical study and discussion at every level *as well as* at forming conscience on the basis of loyalty or obedience. This educational task will mean identifying informed members of the church who are willing to serve the church and the world in this way, and it will mean entering into deliberate dialogue with experts outside our or any other church.

I am suggesting that the church's aim in speaking ought to be primarily to invite and enter into dialogue, in its own ecclesial life and also in its context of a larger culture. This aim might further be described as tending not toward moral regulation but toward moral formation, which I understand as having to do with pedagogy and prophecy, with reflection and action. This requires discovering, examining, and utilizing information and modes of reflection critically and self-critically, in light of our own understanding of ourselves and in light of our understanding of the entirety of the world and the church as created by God and subject to God's judgment and redemption. In other words, one of our aims ought to be to be appropriately informed and formed by those with whom we are in dialogue.

This would suggest that the church ought to speak both to itself and to those who are not members of the church. Our language needs to have several characteristics if in fact it is to be dialogical language which intends to invite and assist in developing consensus. That is, it must be clear: we must "say what we mean and mean what we say."[38] This means, significantly, that we may often wish to use our properly theological and ecclesial language—though not that only—in order to state exactly who we are when we are speaking in the public arena. Second, our language must state clearly what we think we have in common with those with whom we speak, as well as where we differ. Such statements ought, I believe, to recognize the social settings of our speech and the issues I have raised about distribution of power and resources. And our statements ought to indicate to what extent we are willing to reconsider what we have said and why. Other characteristics of dialogical language might be specified as well.

Finally, how binding ought the statements to be? Given the disarray of both church and society, the dialogical approach I am advocating here will mean taking a careful stance about the limits of discussion. We will have to discover and state what we believe, why we believe it, and what consequences for behavior follow from those beliefs. I say this only with the greatest trepidation, because such statements will inevitably describe a set of margins and boundaries for this church, and not necessarily on the basis of justice and reason. Nevertheless, this is a risk we may be willing to undertake if we remember that dialogue with an intent of enlarged vision may legitimately seek to change the consensus.

Finally, such dialogue should be humble, recognizing its theologically-grounded limitations. As James Gustafson has put it, "The voluntary church is Christ's church; but the 'will to belong' does not give a sufficient basis to permit a congregational [or, I might add, denominational] majority to speak for Christ."[39] Our speech ought therefore to be modest and identifiable for what it is. But, I would contend, and for the same reasons, our decisions to keep silence ought to be as carefully and critically made. For not to speak is itself, finally, a form of speech.

Endnotes

1. Allan Parrent above, p. 110.

2. Ibid., pp. 113-115.

3. Ibid., p. 116.

4. For example, Parrent's understanding of the biblical notion of prophecy appears to be based more on a dualism of church-sect than on the biblical record, which allows considerable disparity between prediction and outcome. Biblical prophets are not doom-sayers, but forth-tellers.

5. Timothy Sedgwick above, pp. 74-75.

6. David Scott above, pp. 56-57.

7. Ibid., p. 67.

8. Parrent, pp. 114-115.

9. Stephen W. Sykes, "Introduction: Why Authority?", *Authority in the Anglican Communion: Essays Presented to Bishop John Howe,* Stephen W. Sykes, ed. (Toronto: Anglican Book Centre, 1987), p. 18.

10. See, for example, James M. Gustafson, *The Church as Moral Decision-Maker* (Philadelphia: Pilgrim Press, 1970).

11. Sykes, p. 19; emphasis added.

12. Sykes, p. 19. In the same essay, Sykes quotes a report on the laity from the Canterbury convocation of 1902: "The Church of the apostolic age was neither democratic nor despotic. . . . What it was in general idea may be best expressed by the word 'collective' or 'corporate.' The life and action of the Church were the life and action of the whole body. The officers acted with, not instead of, the community; and the community acted with, not in mere obedience under, its officers. Still less could it supersede or act apart from them. The principle follows directly from the truth that the Holy Spirit was given to the body as a whole. In nothing less than the whole body does the fullness of the Spirit reside—for illumination or for power." (pp. 20–21.)

13. See Gustafson, *The Church as Moral Decision-Maker,* pp. 128ff; and James M. Gustafson, *Protestant and Roman Catholic Ethics* (Chicago: University of Chicago Press, 1978).

14. Gustafson, *Protestant and Roman Catholic Ethics,* pp. 129–130. Gustafson helpfully notes that the moral authority of Protestant teachings is mitigated by factors such as emphasis on work of the Spirit; authoritarian practices (particularly by clergy); theological reasons for not claiming certitude for various teach-

ings; and the fact that accountability finally rests on moral agents themselves, that is, on the "final authority of individual informed conscience" (p. 131).

15. Ibid., p. 130.

16. See Gustafson, *The Church as Moral Decision-Maker*, pp. 109ff.

17. Parrent, p. 115.

18. Gustafson, *The Church as Moral Decision-Maker*, pp. 54–55.

19. John E. Skinner, "Ideology, Authority, and Faith," *Authority in the Anglican Communion*, p. 35. The bracketed phrase comes from another sentence on the same page, and is used there to modify "nurture." Skinner develops his view of authority more fully in his 1983 book *The Meaning of Authority*, which presumably contains the full theological discussion necessary to support such claims.

20. Sykes, p. 13.

21. Skinner, p. 42.

22. Quoted by H.R. McAdoo, "Authority in the Church: Spiritual Freedom and the Corporate Nature of Faith," *Authority in the Anglican Communion*, p. 76; italics in the original. Note the explicit insistence by David Scott and by David Smith and Judith Granbois in this volume on the importance of reason to Anglican identity.

23. Skinner, op. cit.

24. Gustafson, *The Church as Moral Decision-Maker*, p. 154.

25. *The Spiritual Health of the Episcopal Church* (1990), conducted for The Episcopal Church Center by The Gallup Organization, Inc.; distributed by Episcopal Parish Services, Washington, D.C.

26. See on dialogue and conversation David Tracy, *Plurality and Ambiguity: Hermeneutics, Religion, Hope* (San Francisco: Harper and Row, 1987), esp. Chap. 1, "Interpretation, Conversation, Argument."

27. Sedgwick, p. 89.

28. On the importance of power to communicative competence, see the many works of Jürgen Habermas and the theologians who have been influenced by him, such as David Tracy.

29. *The Book of Common Prayer* (1979), p. 518.

30. See, particularly, the many documents produced recently on women in the episcopate. Rightly, these documents refer to the

ordinal. My point here is that they focus on one of the themes found there, to the de-emphasis of others.

31. Sharon D. Welch, *A Feminist Ethic of Risk* (Minneapolis: Fortress Press, 1990), p. 3.

32. Ibid., pp. 20, 21, 75.

33. Ibid., pp. 126, 129.

34. Gustafson, *The Church as Moral Decision-Maker,* p. 132; the pronouns have been changed, *pace* Gustafson.

35. David H. Smith and Judith A. Granbois above, p. 51.

36. Ibid., p. 50.

37. Ibid., p. 51.

38. I have in mind here a rather longer passage from David Tracy's *Plurality and Ambiguity* which addresses the matter of language very well.

39. Gustafson, *The Church as Moral Decision-Maker,* p. 114.

7

How the Church Might Teach

Philip Turner

During the height of the conflict set off by the United States' involvement in the Vietnam War, Paul Ramsey wrote a lengthy criticism of the statement made by the World Council of Churches. Through his criticism Ramsey placed before the churches a question that upset and continues to upset the ecclesiastical powers that be: How can the churches address pressing moral and social issues in a way that allows for legitimate differences of opinion and yet makes clear the ways in which Christian belief illumines the issues at hand?[1]

For anyone who has followed the checkered history of the churches' attempts to speak on public issues, the answer to Ramsey's question is clearly, "Only with great difficulty!" The difficulty is twofold: the moral and social issues are complex, while the theological and moral assumptions that inform judgments are uncritically assumed. These difficulties have produced in all the mainline churches the sort of confusion and loss of credibility that the essays collected in this volume indicate exists within the Episcopal Church.

Many observers have noted both the contradictions and the decline in the moral credibility of church statements. More than a decade ago in *Protestant and Roman Catholic Ethics*, James Gustafson concluded that, in respect to Protestants, "the situation . . . with regard to moral teaching is only a little short of chaos."[2] In his more recent systematic work, *Ethics from a Theocentric Perspective*, he repeated the charge in more explicit terms."What is reprehensible about a great deal of [Protestant] ecclesial moralizing about policy issues is the intellectual and academic flabbiness of most of the pronouncements. . . . The single minded moralism that Protestant churches [more than the Roman Catholic Church] engage in is morally irresponsible."[3] Criticisms like Gustafson's are not

137

unique, but they have failed to alter the tendency of Protestant churches to speak now and think later. The results of this "quick draw" approach to ecclesiastical statements have been disastrous. They force one to ask if there is not a better way for the church as church to speak on matters of public concern.

A better way may be found by addressing a set of questions about ecclesial statements on moral and social issues that have not been asked. Some of these questions are substantive in nature, and some of them are procedural. All are difficult to answer, but this set of questions marks the path Protestant churches must follow if they are to develop a body of moral and social teaching that can garner the respect both of their members and the larger American public.

The Question of Justification

It may be best to begin with the substantive question, "What issues should the church address and why?" This question may be called the question of *justification*. Over the years the Episcopal Church has chosen to make a number of statements about abortion and nuclear weapons. At the present moment it is busy saying, and not saying, a number of things about sexual relations. ECUSA has not, however, chosen to say much about hostile takeovers, programmed trading, in vitro fertilization, or surrogate motherhood. If the churches make a statement on a given issue, what justification can be given for their decision to speak rather than remain silent?

The first question is not whether the church should have spoken on matters about which it has remained silent or whether it should have remained silent on matters upon which it has spoken. The first question is rather on what basis an obligation for ecclesial instruction or advocacy arises in the first place.

There is no single answer to the question of justification. If the church as church makes a claim upon conscience, it must have a good reason for doing so. Furthermore, the reason given for instructing conscience should be other than the intensity of feeling that can be generated at a public meeting by committed advocates. Indeed, it is precisely the question of justification that must be posed if the church is to prevent advocates, filled with passionate intensity, from capturing its institutions and organs of speech and then creating the impression either that they speak for the entire church or that they ought to.

No better example of the importance of attending adequately to the question of justification can be found than that of the Episcopal Church's response to the abortion debate.[4] The first statement on abortion made by the General Convention was in 1967, prior to the decision of the Supreme Court in the case of *Roe v. Wade*. The concern of that statement was whether or not the church ought to support changes in the laws governing abortion in the various states. The first proposal which came before the House of Bishops contained a brief theological justification for what was said. This proposal said that the church has an obligation to speak because "the sanctity of human life is of paramount concern in Christian theology and teaching."[5]

Whatever one may think of this justification, the first proposal before the House of Bishops provided a theological warrant for an ecclesiastical statement on abortion. In its place, however, the bishops accepted a more pragmatic reason for addressing the issue, namely that "Abortion law reform has become, or will become, a legislative issue in virtually all the fifty states, inevitably raising questions on which the guidance of the Church is sought."[6] With this pragmatic justification the resolution was sent to the House of Deputies. It is important to note that the resolution placed by the bishops before the House of Deputies removed all reference to Christian warrants for addressing abortion. Instead, the resolution was justified on the very questionable basis that the church was obliged to speak on abortion because a number of people expected it to do so.

With the benefit of hindsight, it can be seen that the refusal of the bishops to provide a theological warrant for the church as church to speak proved disastrous. During the course of the convention, the resolution addressing abortion law reform was further revised until the reason the church had to speak was neither for specifically Christian reasons nor because people expected it to do so. The warrant for addressing abortion became weaker still. The final form of the resolution which issued from the House of Deputies, a form to which the bishops later assented, contained as its justification the notation that "Several Diocese of the Episcopal Church have joined with civic, social, and welfare groups in urging that state laws governing abortion be amended along lines recommended by the American Law Institute and the American Medical Association."[7]

The warrant for an ecclesiastical statement on abortion became simply that two interested professional associations and an unstated number of dioceses found themselves in agreement that some change in the laws of the various states was necessary. Why, it must be asked, is this a reason for the church to speak its mind, or for anyone, especially one who may not agree with the several dioceses, the American Law Institute, and the American Medical Association, to give heed to what the church may have to say? In part, the statement of the 1967 Convention has had so little authority because of the weakness of its justification. Indeed, the justification given in 1967 was so weak that by 1988 a completely different justification and a completely different resolution proved to be necessary.

By 1988, as a result of the decision of the Supreme Court in the case of *Roe v. Wade*, abortion on demand had become legal. In response to these circumstances the General Convention spoke not about legal reform but about the morality of abortion itself. Further, it spoke not to the nation as a whole but to members of the Episcopal Church alone. The resolution of General Convention gave as a justification for the church's teaching (1) a belief on the part of Christians in the "sacredness of human life," and (2) the obligation of the church "to help form the consciences of its members concerning this sacredness."[8] After twenty years of debate and struggle a justification that at least approaches a theological one has emerged from ECUSA's governing body. The justification provided is, however, both brief and inadequate. What makes *human* life sacred, and why is it that only members of ECUSA are to be instructed about this sacredness?

This brief review of the course of the abortion debate within the Episcopal Church forces one to conclude that ECUSA has yet to provide either its members or the general public an adequate justification for its attempts to guide both conscience and public policy in respect to abortion. The church may indeed have authority to instruct the conscience of its members, and it may have a responsibility to speak to the consciences of all people. It cannot do so rightly or successfully, however, unless it can show that it has a reason for speaking that accords both with an adequate articulation of Christian belief and practice and with the demands of right reason.

The Purpose of Moral Teachings

The second of the questions that ought to be asked before the church undertakes to speak is, "What ought the purpose of a statement to be?" The question of purpose is rarely asked directly for the simple reason that many assume the purpose of ecclesial statements to be obvious. In recent years, certainly since the mid-1960s, it has been assumed that the church in both its speech and action ought to be prophetic and advocatory. That is to say, in making statements on public issues, the church as church ought to expose and denounce particular moral and social ills and advocate particular policies in order to remedy those ills.

Many examples of the prophetic/advocatory aim can be found. The statements about war and nuclear weapons made since 1979 by ECUSA's House of Bishops are among the clearest. Allan Parrent has traced what the bishops have said through their resolutions and in their pastoral letters. Their statements supported, among other things, a nuclear freeze. They also opposed both the deployment of intermediate range missiles in Europe and the expenditure of large sums of money for more advanced weaponry. The bishops' statements have been prophetic in that they have denounced military policy and decried spending monies for weaponry that ought to have been spent "to meet human needs." They have been advocatory in that they have supported particular military, political, and social policy alternatives on the basis that such policies were morally acceptable in ways that the actual policies of the government were not.

When reading the bishops' statements, one cannot miss the moral seriousness of their purpose. Nevertheless, Parrent's analysis of their statements leads him to conclude that their attempts at both prophecy and advocacy leave much to be desired. Thus he points out that had the policy advocacy of the bishops succeeded, (1) the balance of power in Europe would have shifted in a way that destabilized the military and political situation, (2) the present more favorable situation in regard to Eastern Europe would not have come about, and (3) the military budget would have risen in order to increase the conventional forces which would have been needed in the absence of a convincing nuclear deterrent. Parrent goes on to make the point that the way in which the bishops made prophetic statements on behalf of human need implied that defense was not one of those needs and had no moral place in the assessment of public policies.

Parrent's assessment of the church's teaching on war and nuclear weapons leads him to caution the church "in its use of the word prophetic, especially as applied to itself." He goes on to say:

The word prophetic . . . is sometimes used rather too glibly to refer to positions which individuals happen to like, which safely appeal to the proclivities of an audience, or which seem the most radical and therefore supposedly the most authentic. Such statements may in fact be prophetic. But they may also be misuses of the term in order to undergird predetermined ideological views or to give religious respectability to what may in fact be irrational or irresponsible. The prophetic is often proclaimed too easily because the prophet bears no responsibility for the relevant decision or its consequences.[9]

Not only have such prophetic statements often appeared in retrospect to be little more than "simplistic moralizing" or attempts to "undergird predetermined ideological views," they have also appeared to fault the consciences of those who have different but defensible judgments on what ought to be done.

It can and has been asked if the aim of church statements on public affairs ought to be less prophetic and more pedagogical. To be more precise, ought the church when it speaks its mind to aim at prophecy and advocacy of particular policies? Instead, ought the church to aim at informing the members of the church about Christian belief and about public matters in light of those beliefs? It is the first of these aims that informed the Convention statement on abortion in 1967, but it is the second that is reflected in the statement of 1988. The records of the Conventions of 1967 and 1988 show that these Conventions had very different purposes in speaking, one prophetic and the other pedagogical.

While it is one thing for an individual to have a "prophetic calling," for an entire people or nation to be prophetic is something rather different. There are individuals who get a fire in the belly that won't go away. They are irresistibly called to expose the wrongs perpetrated by their people and to call them back to the foundations of their religious and moral life. Properly speaking, prophets are individuals who have no choice but to speak about the evil they see and to call people back to their roots. Time alone tells if what they have seen is truth or falsehood.

Communities of people, however, cannot be prophets in the same way individuals can. Groups have no sudden and irresistible call. Their call is mediated through the call of the prophetic individual. Groups are called to obey the prophet's "word" and, in so doing, become prophetic in a more derivative sense. The way of life that may result from obeying the prophet's call, by its example, can be prophetic in the sense that the light it reflects may well expose the surrounding darkness and show at the same time an alternative way to go about life's business. Thus, one might say that the care given by the early church to its own poor showed obedience to Christ's prophetic word and at the same time served as a prophetic example for both Christians, Jews, and Gentiles.

If these observations are correct, the instructional and prophetic aims which now seem opposed ought in fact to be seen as necessary one to another. How can there be a common way of life that serves as a prophetic example if the members of the church do not share a common vision and way of life, and how can there be a common vision and way of life if there is no instruction of conscience? Furthermore, how can the adequacy of instruction be measured save by the lives changed by its force. A prophetic witness by an ecclesial institution is possible only if the church forms a people whose lives reflect what is said. In turn, the lives of the people can reflect what is said only if adequate instruction has been given about a common foundation upon which the life of the people is based. It is difficult to imagine how a church can be prophetic if it is not first of all instructional, and it is difficult to imagine how the church can escape being prophetic if it is faithful in the instruction it offers.

Church officials who undertake to speak for the church ought to have as their chief aim the instruction of the church. Given this aim, it ought to be their hope to form a common life that serves as a prophetic witness. However, no matter what the results of their efforts, the question remains whether or not the church ought ever to advocate particular policies in response to public issues.

In the latter part of the nineteenth century and for the first half of the twentieth, both Roman Catholic and Protestant churches assumed that the aim of their social teaching ought to be to state, in general terms, the nature of the good of society and then to leave the determination of particular policies to individual consciences. For both, policy determination was a matter of prudence, and the determination of what is prudent was thought to be a matter over which people of both good will and intelligence could rightly disagree. In the 1950s, however, Protestant social teaching began to move in a more specific direction. In both Europe and the United States, churches began to think that general instruction about the good of society remained too far above the real issues of political life. What was needed was more specific instruction about how Christians and others ought to view particular political alternatives. For example, John Bennett argued that the church in its instruction ought to propose "middle axioms" or "proximate goals" at which Christians and others ought to aim, although the church should avoid particular policy advocacy.[10]

The suggestions of Bennett proved popular for a time, but at the 1966 conference on church and society, sponsored by the World Council of Churches, a dramatic move to advocacy occurred. At that conference the delegates voted in support of particular policy solutions to the Vietnam War. Their action was followed both in this country and abroad by other ecumenical bodies and by the governing bodies of particular churches. Since that time the Protestant churches as a whole have turned away from the debate they carried on in the early part of the century about the nature of the social good. Instead, they have increasingly criticized particular social policies and espoused others. Though it came a bit later and is less pronounced, a similar move can be traced within American Catholicism and within the more evangelical Protestant churches.

The question is whether or not these attempts at prophecy and advocacy represent an adequate understanding of what a faithful response on the part of the church as church ought to involve. The record of what the churches have had to say about public affairs, as Gustafson charges, shows that the Protestants have spoken hastily and without sufficient thought. But ought they to have espoused the prophetic/advocatory aim in the first place? This is a more fundamental issue than the adequacy of what they have had to say.

There are two powerful arguments that can be made against the shift away from pedagogy and toward prophetic advocacy. The first is that the espousal of particular policy options by a church as church suggests that on a given issue there is only one possible position about policy that Christians can hold. Political judgment does not lend itself to this sort of certainty. For example, from a Christian perspective a good society may be viewed as one in which racial difference is not used as a means to deny people equal access to the benefits of social and political life. It does not follow, however, that court-ordered busing or quotas in hiring are the best ways to rectify a situation in which the sharing of benefits is unjustly distributed because of racial prejudice.

The second point follows from the first. If Christians may rightly disagree about the particulars of social policy, then insistence that Christians espouse one policy option rather than another introduces divisions within the life of the church which have no justifiable place there. That is, if Christians as Christians may rightly disagree, not about racial equality but about the best way to achieve it, then policy advocacy on this matter divides the church in a way not occasioned by a necessary defense of the truth of the gospel. Thus, policy advocacy may be a sin by the church as church against the unity of the church itself, rather than a faithful and prophetic act by the church as church for the sake of the church and the world. This is a charge that infuriates many, but, nevertheless, ought not to be summarily dismissed.

Policy advocacy has its problems. In politics, what we are certain of today may tomorrow prove illusory, unwise, or even wicked. Still, even as vocal a critic of ecclesial prophecy and advocacy as Paul Ramsey was forced in his later writings to say that prohibiting the discussion of particular policy options placed too much of a restriction upon the teaching function of the bishops of his own church.[11] If you will, discussions of the social good of peace and good will among nations or of racial equality within nations that exclude the consideration of particular policies float above the fray. More significantly, such discussions prevent the church from exercising its responsibility for instructing the conscience of its members about what Christian belief in fact implies for social and political life. Thus Ramsey concluded that even a policy statement like that made by the archbishop of Canterbury on the occasion of the war England fought with Argentina over the Falkland Islands did not go far enough in the direction of particular policy discussions. The statement said simply that the government's actions in the Falklands would not "fail to find Christian support." Ramsey's point was that if it is not enough to speak only in general terms about social good, it is also not enough to say only that a given policy is one that Christians may support, though they need not.

Ramsey went on to argue that a more specific discussion of both social goods and particular policy options is necessary if the churches are to fulfill their obligations in respect to social teaching. The problem is how to do this without implying that there is but one morally defensible policy option. Ramsey's conclusion was that when Christians reach what he called "a fork in the road beyond which they cannot proceed by clear Christian warrant," the churches ought to explore all the policy roads that might branch out from that fork. In this way all the issues will in time be exposed. As a consequence the churches can give responsible instruction about real political life. At the same time, however, they can avoid faulting the policy views of some while giving undue support to the views of others. In exploring the range of policies addressing an issue, all the voices in the church can be heard; in the process, though, everyone who chooses to speak will be "forced back upon their presuppositions" and so required to give an adequate defense of the position they have espoused.[12] A procedure like this might well reveal some policies that ought not to be espoused. Such a procedure also has a better chance of maintaining a unity within the church that is built upon both truth and love, rather than upon a political victory by one party over another.

What I have called the question of purpose has revealed two additional issues. One is the question of content. What exactly ought the churches to say about a particular issue when they decide they have good reason to speak? The second issue is the question of procedure. How in deciding what needs to be said can discussion proceed in a way that ensures that all the voices in the church are heard, that the church speaks from clear Christian warrants, and that the implications of those warrants for political life are adequately developed? The argument to this point suggests that contrary to present practice, the questions of justification, purpose, and procedure ought all to precede the question of content. That is, before any attempt is made to articulate a specific statement on a matter of public concern, the church as church must ask itself why it has an obligation to speak, what its aim in speaking ought to be, and how it ought to go about finding out what needs to be said.

There are several other questions that ought to precede the rush to specify the particular content of the teachings of the church. The four of the most immediate concern are: (1) to whom ought the churches address themselves, (2) in what language ought they to speak, (3) in what form ought they to express themselves, and (4) who ought to do the talking?

To Whom Ought the Church Speak?

First, there is the question of audience. In addressing moral, social, and political issues, ought the church to direct what it says to its own members only or ought it to direct itself as well to members of the general public? That the Episcopal Church has not asked this question with any degree of consistency and rigor becomes clear if one traces once more the history of the General Convention resolutions on the matter of abortion. In 1967 the resolution of the General Convention appears, as David Scott has said, "to address no one in particular."[13] It presupposes that ECUSA has a responsibility to speak not only to its own membership but to the nation as a whole. In view of this assumption, it is startling to note that the resolution on abortion passed by the Convention of 1988 is addressed only to members of the Episcopal Church. Is ECUSA, as suggested by the resolution of 1967, to continue in the tradition of the national churches spawned at the Reformation and so seek to provide the moral basis for national life? In contrast, as suggested by the resolution of 1988, is the Episcopal Church to close ranks, focus on its own internal life, and so seek, by means of example, to make a witness in the midst of an alien, perhaps even hostile, social order?

Examples of the church relating to the social order as the soul of the nation or as a faithful community in an alien world are both to be found in the history of this nation. Nevertheless, in considering which option the Episcopal Church ought to take, Episcopalians should note carefully what Parrent has said about the dominant tradition within Anglicanism and the other mainline Protestant churches. That tradition has stressed the role both of the churches and of individual Christians in the general moral and political life of society. In view of the moral vacuum now present in what Richard Neuhaus has nicely called "the naked public square," Parrent sees a need to reassert that tradition against the sort of sectarian tendencies that might be reflected in the 1988 resolution on abortion.[14]

Parrent's admonitions are timely but require amplification. When Thomas Cranmer wrote the first versions of the *Book of Common Prayer*, he assumed the existence of a Christian society. Cranmer, like Calvin and Luther, was heir to the agreement between church and empire struck under the emperor Constantine. In return for the provision of a unifying religious and moral base for the empire, the church was given special place and special privilege within the body politic. What is now called pluralism was exactly that social phenomenon the church was supposed to combat rather than support. Accordingly, during each celebration of Holy Communion, the people were to pray on behalf of the commonwealth that the sovereign would rule in a way that served both the promotion of "true religion and virtue" and the punishment of "wickedness and vice." What constituted true religion and virtue and what constituted wickedness and vice were not matters to be determined by private judgment but by the church. Further, once the church had determined the content of true religion and virtue, both were to be enforced by public authority.

Whether one looks left, right, or center, much of the present drive for the churches to have something to say on all matters of public interest stems from an established church mentality. In the minds of many liberals and conservatives, the church must speak on public affairs to all and sundry so that society as a whole will be based firmly upon Christian beliefs and the moral practices implied by those beliefs. From this perspective, the government is to protect the churches' right to speak and to enact laws which promote the beliefs and practices which the churches support. However, as reflected in the changing reasons in the Episcopal Church for addressing abortion, an increasing number of persons believe that the churches cannot and ought not to serve as moral tutor for American society. The churches instead inevitably turn inward. Nevertheless, Parrent seems right when he says that the more public tradition of the mainline churches needs to be reasserted rather than deserted. The question is, of course, how can churches as churches serve the common good of pluralistic and democratic society?

At the least, churches have no chance of offering effective moral instruction to the general population if they have not first succeeded in instructing those of their own members. If the lives of their members do not accord to some extent with the teaching of the church, there is no way for the churches to speak in a way that will gain attention. This is especially the case if the moral beliefs and practices of the churches are at odds with the beliefs and practices of the environing culture. As an example, the resolution of the 1988 General Convention on abortion is right as far as it goes. It rightly recognizes the need of the churches in a pluralistic society to maintain the integrity of Christian belief and practice. It is inadequate, however, in that it remains silent about any obligation the churches might have to address people who live their lives apart from the body of the church.

The Question of Language

If the churches continue to address both their own members and society as a whole, a reconsideration of what might be called the question of language is also necessary. If, for example, as the Episcopal Church has asserted, people ought to refrain from the practice of abortion as a means of birth control, how is the church to justify such a moral claim either to its own membership or to the public at large? In what moral language is the church to make its appeal for adherence to a teaching that is at odds with common practice and the law of the land? Should the church appeal to Christian warrants alone or must it make reference as well to moral notions which do not have specifically Christian origins or specifically Christian content?

The question of language is not one that has an obvious answer. If the audience addressed by the churches is comprised only of church members, then it may be sensible and sufficient for the churches to justify their moral teaching by use of a uniquely Christian moral vocabulary. For example, in speaking to church members about race relations, the nature of the kingdom of God can and ought to be cited as a good reason to seek changes in the policies and laws that uphold a social pattern of racial segregation. If, however, the audience addressed is wider than the churches' membership, the churches may appropriately make a more universal appeal by using moral language which is not specifically Christian: for example, the language of equal rights. It is equally sensible, however, to ask if in order to make their witness clear the churches ought to speak to one and all only in Christian terms. And, of course, in order both to bear witness and to make a general appeal to right reason, churches may employ a variety of moral vocabularies: for example, a combination of kingdom language and rights language.

Although the answer to the question of language is not obvious, the church has not had much debate about the language to be used in its teaching. Still, the question of language lies just below the surface of the actual debates on what is to be said. In fact, the question that most bitterly divides the right and left wings within the churches is the question of language, for the simple reason that the language used reveals theological understandings and assumptions. More broadly, it is clarifying to note that different languages are used by different churches and organizations. For example, the social pronouncements of the World Council of Churches have, on the whole, been expressed in the specifically Christian language of the reign of God. The social encyclicals of the Roman Catholic Church use the more universal language of natural law into which the modern idiom of human rights has been incorporated.

Behind these differences in the language used in teaching lie conflicting ways in which to construe Christian belief. These differences need to be more clearly stated and more directly addressed if much progress is to be made in the articulation of ecclesiastical moral and social teaching. Attention to the question of language, should it come, will certainly spark a lively ecumenical debate. Further, if this debate occurs, it would not be foolish to suppose that the mainline churches will seek a mediating position, one perhaps that argues for some combination of the language of the kingdom and the language of rights.

The most adequate answer to the question of language may well prove to be the mediating one. It seems sensible, after all, to call both for a specifically Christian witness and for an attempt on the part of the churches to recommend what they have to say by showing that their views are not only Christian but also in accord with what society might come to recognize as right reason. It may prove sanguine, however, to espouse the middle way too quickly. Mediating positions are always attractive but not always defensible. They are attractive because they hold out the promise of including the best of all positions. However, they may also prove a snare and elusion, an invitation to compromise that results in a sort of "Babylonian captivity of the church." The result of such a captivity is the secularization of Christian beliefs and forms of life and assimilation into an alien worldview. For a church whose tradition seeks to speak to the common good, this danger is altogether too real.

How Should the Church Speak?

The most adequate answer to the question of language is far from obvious, but even if that answer could be determined another dilemma presents itself, namely, the question of the form of communication. Harmon Smith's paper on what the Episcopal Church has had to say about marriage and sexual relationships poses the issue of the form of communication rather nicely. He suggests that one form in which the church might offer moral instruction is that of the dialogue. Dialogue is suited to bring out the relative strengths and weaknesses of a variety of points of view. It allows everyone to have their say and rules out no position from the beginning.

The dialogue is a form of public speech that is understandably popular in a society that is committed to democratic pluralism. In this type of social order, all opinions are supposedly allowed. The misunderstandings and conflicts that may accompany such pluralism are mitigated by a constant process of dialogue that serves to further mutual understanding and the toleration of difference.

Smith suggests, with more than a touch of irony, that in order to fit in easily with its social environment, the Episcopal Church is in fact adopting the dialogical form as a favored means to provide instruction on both moral and public policy issues. As a result, the attempts of its General Convention and the House of Bishops to provide moral and social teaching remind one on occasion of the Joan Rivers' show. As does Joan in her imaginary conversations, members of the Episcopal Church in their discussion of public issues constantly repeat the formula one to another: "Hey, can we talk?" This invitation is repeated endlessly during the course of the church's meetings. As a result, positions may be clarified, but no conclusions need be reached.[15]

Smith's irony suggests that there may be problems with a church whose only means of instruction is endless conversation. Chief among these is that dialogue in and of itself has no means of closure. The open-ended character of the dialogue well suits it for the investigation of disputed issues. It may, therefore, rightly be used in perpetuity for the discussion of questions that ought not to receive or cannot be given a definitive answer. However, churches have taught through the ages that there are certain things that Christians ought not to believe and that there are certain forms of behavior not open to them. There are certain questions that, for the sake of the truth about Christ and the integrity of the church's common life, require some form of closure. Though dialogue will serve well the process of investigation required before an adequate conclusion can be reached, dialogue will not serve as a means for expressing the church's mind on a disputed question once that mind is made up.

In contrast to dialogue, churches have addressed beliefs and practices through canons, resolutions, and more fully developed documents such as pastoral letters or commission reports. Member churches of the Anglican communion have avoided, if possible, the use of canons as a means of instructing conscience. Only on rare occasions—for example, divorce, rebellion, regicide, and treason—have canons been used to place a moral claim upon the political behavior of church members. Anglicans have felt, on the whole, that to cast decisions in the form of canon law limits the pastoral practice of the church and inadvisedly entangles the church in the discipline of the lives of its individual members.

Recognizing the inadequacies of canon law, the Episcopal Church has in recent years made increasing use of the resolution. The resolution is an apt form for delegates to a convention to express the majority opinion. Resolutions, however, are of limited use as a means for ordering the common life of the church. The authority of resolutions is unclear, and they are of little value as a means for the instruction of conscience. Instruction must aim at the assent of conscience, but assent requires free acceptance based on conviction. Conviction, moreover, cannot be expected apart from justifying arguments. It is just this reasoned defense that the resolution cannot provide. A list of "whereas" clauses followed by the phrase "therefore, be it resolved" is not a form of communication designed to convince. It can do no more than identify issues and announce or pronounce a conclusion. In part, because mainline churches have sought to articulate moral and social teaching solely by the pronouncement of conclusions not widely shared, their attempts at the formation of conscience through resolutions have proved both futile and divisive.

There are forms of communication better suited to teaching than either the canon or the resolution, namely, reports and pastoral letters. The report can marshal in one place large amounts of information and can also present within a single cover the various sides of an issue. A good example of such reports is the work of the Church of England's Board for Social

Responsibility on such topics as marriage, homosexuality, euthanasia, the homeless, and prisons.[16]

The pastoral letter as a means of reasoned instruction is well illustrated by the significant impact on public debate made by the pastoral letters on war and the economy published in recent years by the National Conference of Catholic Bishops.[17] These letters have by no means won universal assent, but they have gained a wide audience because of their reasoned appeal to conscience. Personal commitment, clear statement, and careful justification are characteristics that serve at the same time to convey the authority of those who undertake to instruct the mind of the churches, to respect the liberty of those reading the letter, and to recommend the teaching of the churches both to mind and heart.

Who Should Speak?

Individual members in their daily lives are the primary agents through whom the churches speak on matters of public concern. For better and for worse, the churches make their voices heard most powerfully through the lives of their members. For this reason, it is easy to understand why the churches rarely speak with a single voice. In a more immediate sense, however, one still must ask who is to speak when the church as church sees a need to instruct conscience and form behavior in respect to a particular matter of moral concern or public policy. This issue may be called the question of agency.

In the Episcopal Church there are many agents who might have spoken for the church on the issues that in recent years have come before it. In addition to the General Convention, there are, for example, the House of Bishops, executive officers, standing commissions, voluntary societies, religious orders, congregations, vestries, rectors, theologians, and seminary faculties. In the Episcopal Church and in other Protestant churches, however, legislative bodies have been the primary agents to speak for the church. The pronouncements of these bodies have become so common that few church members even stop to ask if a legislative body is the right agent either to instruct the church or to address the world on their behalf.

Given the many alternatives and the poor performance of legislative bodies, one is forced to ask if they are the best agents to speak for the church. In his reply to a statement made by Methodist bishops on war and nuclear weapons, Paul

Ramsey asked if bodies that meet for ten days to two weeks every three or four years are indeed suited to speak on complex moral and social issues. He went on to suggest that his church might consider employing others to speak for the church.[18] Similar observations and suggestions seem apt in the case of the Episcopal Church.

Still, who should be charged to speak for the church on any given occasion? The principle to be used in answering the question is easy to state though difficult to apply. The principle is that the agent that ought to speak for the church should be determined on the basis of the purpose of what is to be said. If the purpose is to instruct conscience, to pass a law, to discipline members, or to address the general public, then the agent charged under the constitution of the church with the particular responsibility in question ought to speak. To assume otherwise is to court either the usurpation of authority or its renunciation.

How to Proceed

Assigning responsibility in a given situation for a particular agent to speak does not imply that an individual or a body of the church ought to speak without reference to the church as a whole. Without extensive prayer, study, and consultation, no one can in fact speak for the church. This returns us again to the question of procedure.

In light of what has been said to this point, in order to speak for the church there must first be discussions that ensure (1) that all the voices in the church are given an opportunity to speak and to be heard, (2) that the right agent is charged with the responsibility for deciding what needs to be said and saying it, and (3) that the Christian warrants for what may be said are developed in a way that adequately reflects the implications of those warrants for moral and political life. Even this brief description suggests how fearfully complex is the question of procedure.

The most successful procedure to emerge in recent years is that of the Roman Catholic Church. Draft pastoral letters are prepared by the Vatican or by a conference of bishops. These drafts are circulated for comment, not only to the general membership of the church but also to theologians and others who can provide expert opinion. Then the letters are redrafted and recirculated. This process continues until the persons responsible for the final form letter think the process of consultation has gone as far as it needs to go. A final version of the pastoral letter is then prepared and published as the basis for teaching throughout the church.

The procedure used in the Roman Catholic church has served to create statements on moral and public policy issues that are of the highest quality. Nevertheless, as the encyclical *Humanae Vitae* clearly illustrates, the authority invested by the Roman Church in its teaching office is such that the instruction given may in the end ignore the wisdom of the church itself. As John Mahoney has shown, in *Humanae Vitae* Pope Paul VI took a stance that went contrary both to the views of a majority of faithful Catholics and to the judgments of moral theologians and other expert witnesses.[19] In speaking both to the church and to the world on the subject of contraception, Paul VI may well have done so in a way that failed to speak for the church. For different reasons the pronouncements from the synods, conventions, and meetings of the Protestant churches also have spoken both to the church and to the world in a way that does not speak for the church. In the particular case of the Episcopal Church, its statements on war, abortion, and other matters have failed to be informed by either popular or expert opinion.

Pronouncements of the Episcopal Church have emerged in a way that obscures who speaks and on what authority. Does the authority of a pronouncement rest in the General Convention, in the House of Bishops, or elsewhere? To say, as often is the case, that teaching authority is dispersed simply begs the question, unless one wants in the end to say that no agent has been invested by the church with the authority to speak for the church on questions of conscience. If, however, no one speaks for the church, then what are the churches doing when they appear to ask a synod, convention, or particular body of ecclesial functionaries to speak on their behalf?

The last observation displays the most difficult issue now facing the Episcopal Church. As Ephraim Radner and George Sumner have pointed out, at the heart of many of the disputed moral and social issues before the church lie profound disputes over doctrine. The sad fact is that the Episcopal Church has no way at the moment to resolve these doctrinal issues.[20] At the time of the Reformation, the Church of England asserted the right to determine matters of church order and liturgy on the basis of local requirements. Matters of doctrine, however, were not to be considered matters of local discretion. In respect to these issues, the Church of England did not resort to confessions, as did their Lutheran and Calvinist companions. Rather, they insisted that matters of doctrine are to be determined in accord with the witness of Holy Scripture and the decisions of the ecumenical councils of the church. When matters of faith and morals become matters of dispute only an ecumenical council can make a definitive determination of what must be believed and done. This rather conservative premise has worked fairly well because of the restraint of the English people. It is not, however, working well in the United States. Americans are a litigious people who more and more are inclined to press their own point of view as far as possible. In such circumstances the traditional restraints on disputed questions become increasingly unintelligible.

For American Episcopalians, the need to press particular points of view and the increasing absence of taken-for-granted understandings and assumptions place severe strains upon their polity. The General Convention provides both a way to change church order and liturgy to suit local needs and opinions. It is a medium by means of which various factions can press their points of view. General Convention does not, however, provide an adequate way to resolve disputes over faith and morals. Such is not the constitutional purpose of the General Convention. Consequently, Episcopalians have no clear way to tackle the more fundamental issues that confront them. Their cultural circumstances make it impossible for them to wait for an ecumenical council to resolve matters in dispute, and it would be contrary to their tradition to write a new confession that would resolve disputed issues. They are, therefore, simply thrown back upon an inappropriate means. The political struggles and resolutions of General Convention are the only means they have to address differences. These unsuitable means to resolve disputed matters of doctrine and practice, moreover, exacerbate their divisions.

The Question of Reception
For individuals the questions raised above regarding the church and its teaching may pose a pressing matter of conscience. If the church speaks, is there any obligation for people in the church and for those outside the church to listen to what has been said? This issue may be called the question of reception.

For members of the church, it seems reasonable to say that

there are circumstances under which Christians have both a religious and moral obligation not only to listen when their church speaks but also to regard what is said as having a prima facie claim upon conscience. The obliging conditions are just those mentioned above. If the procedures have been followed which allow for all views to be expressed and for each party to the debate to be "forced back upon their presuppositions," and if the questions of justification, purpose, audience, language, form of communication, and agency have been asked and answered, then one must assume that opportunity has been given for the Spirit of God to lead the church into truth. If these conditions are not present, then one need make no such assumption. In the first instance, the burden of proof lies with the individual if one finds oneself in disagreement with what the church has said. In the second instance, no such obligation is present since the agent of the church who speaks for the church has failed to do what is required to discover "the mind of Christ" for the church.

The question of reception is more difficult when it is posed in relation to those outside the church, to the general public. Indeed, it seems odd even to ask if people who do not belong to the church have an obligation to listen when the church speaks. In the United States there is no established religion and so no civil obligation either to support or to accept the teachings or discipline of any religious group. Nevertheless, there is within democratic society a prima facie obligation on the part of the citizenry not only to allow other people to state their views but also to give those views a fair hearing. In this sense, there is a civic duty to listen when churches speak, just as there is a civic duty to listen when any other person or group speaks. There is, however, no duty to place the burden of proof on oneself if one happens to disagree with what is being said.

In a pluralistic and democratic society, when the church decides to speak to the general public on a matter of morals or social policy, the authority of their statements is only as strong as the case they make. Ecclesial statements on public issues must make their way in the public square on the basis of their power to convince. They can make no privileged claim upon conscience. Therefore, in a pluralistic society, public acceptance of ecclesial teaching can come about in but three ways: by the power of example, by the power of argument, or by some combination of the two. None of these are likely if the churches bypass the questions that have been out-lined in the body of this paper. To make the same point rather more bluntly, if the churches in the United States are to be pedagogical and so also prophetic, they must first take steps to ensure that they are in fact behaving like churches.

Endnotes

1. Paul Ramsey, *Who Speaks for the Church? A Critique of the 1966 Geneva Conference on Church and Society* (Nashville: Abingdon, 1967).

2. James Gustafson, *Protestant and Roman Catholic Ethics* (Chicago: University of Chicago Press, 1978), p. 130.

3. James Gustafson, *Ethics from a Theocentric Perspective* Vol. II (Chicago: University of Chicago Press, 1984), p. 318.

4. For detailed studies of the course of this debate see David Scott above and Philip Turner, "Social Advocacy as a Moral Issue in Itself," *The Journal of Religious Ethics,* Vol. 19 (Fall 1991)2: pp. 157–181.

5. *Journal of the General Convention,* 1967, p. 307. The con-stitution of ECUSA provides for a General Convention whose delegates are divided into two houses. The House of Deputies is comprised of lay people and clergy. The House of Bishops is comprised of all the bishops of the church. For an action to become an action of the General Convention, it must pass both houses.

6. Ibid.

7. Ibid.

8. *The Journal of the General Convention,* 1988, p. 633; see above pp. 72–73.

9. See Allan Parrent above, p. 113.

10. See, for example, John C. Bennett, *The Christian as Citizen,* World Christian Books No. 5 (London: Lutterworth, 1955), pp. 39–41.

11. See, for example, Paul Ramsey, *Speak Up for Just War or Pacifism* (Nashville: Abingdon, 1988), p. 132.

12. For Ramsey's presentation of these views see *Speak Up for Just War or Pacifism,* pp. 125–147.

13. See Scott above, p. 61.

14. See Parrent above, pp. 114–115.

15. See Harmon Smith above, p. 16.

16. See Timothy Sedgwick above, p. 92–93, note 35.

17. See the National Conference of Catholic Bishops, *The Challenge of Peace* (Washington: U.S. Catholic Conference, 1983) and the National Conference of Catholic Bishops, *Economic Justice for All* (Washington: U.S. Catholic Conference, 1986).

18. Paul Ramsey, *Speak Up for Just War or Pacifism*, pp. 13, 135.

19. See John Mahoney, S.J., *The Making of Moral Theology: A Study of the Roman Catholic Tradition* (Oxford: Clarendon, 1987), pp. 259–274.

20. See Ephraim Radner and George Sumner, Jr., "Waiting on the Spirit: Episcopalians and Homosexuality," *The Christian Century* (9 October 1991), pp. 910–913.